Nevada Public Library
631 K Avenue
Nevada, IA 50201
515-382-2628

AMERICAN STREET

AMERICAN STREET

IBI ZOBOI

BALZER + BRAY
An Imprint of HarperCollins*Publishers*

Balzer + Bray is an imprint of HarperCollins Publishers.

American Street
Copyright © 2017 by Alloy Entertainment and Ibi Zoboi

ISBN 978-0-06-247304-2 (trade bdg.)

Typography by Liz Dresner

17 18 19 20 21   PC/LSCH   10 9 8

❖

First Edition

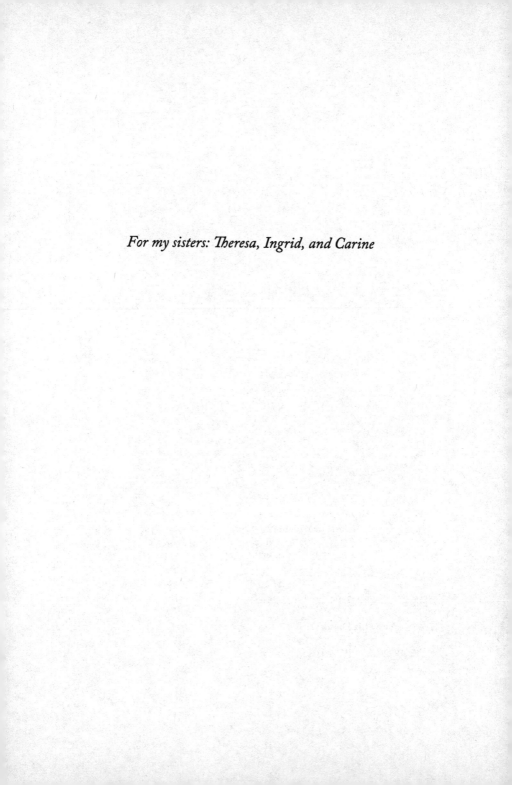

For my sisters: Theresa, Ingrid, and Carine

ONE

IF ONLY I could break the glass separating me and Manman with my thoughts alone. On one side of the glass doors are the long lines of people with their photos and papers that prove that they belong here in America, that they are allowed to taste a bit of this free air. On the other side is me, pressing my forehead against the thick see-through wall. My shoulder hurts from the weight of the carry-on bag. I refuse to put it down for fear that they will take it away, too.

"Manman," I whisper to the glass, hoping that my voice will ease through, fly above all those people's heads, travel on a plane back to New York, and reach her.

We had been holding hands for courage when we arrived at Customs in Kennedy Airport. Manman had carried all our important documents in a big yellow envelope tucked into her large purse—our passports, her visa, and the papers to prove that we are who we say we are, that we are from the city of Port-au-Prince; that I am an American citizen by birth and I left for good when I was only an infant; that we own a little house in the neighborhood of Delmas; and that Manman has a business selling brand-name *pépé*—secondhand American clothes. All these things to prove that we are only visiting relatives and plan to return home to Haiti.

But how could they have read our minds? How could they have known that my mother's big sister in Detroit had been sending us money to leave Haiti forever? How could they have known that we didn't plan to go back?

"Ms. Valerie Toussaint, I need you to come with me," the man had said. His voice was like the pebbled streets in Delmas, rough and unsteady as they pulled Manman's hand from mine; as they motioned for me to continue through the line with Manman's desperate pleas trailing behind me—*Alé, Fabiola! Go, Fabiola! Don't worry. I will meet you there!*—and as I got on the connecting flight from New York to Detroit. But too much has happened for me to cry now. On the plane ride leaving Port-au-Prince for JFK, I had curled into my mother and together we looked out the window. Up high in the sky, all the problems we had left behind seemed so tiny—as if I could pick them up one by one and fling them out of the universe.

On the flight to Detroit, I am alone. I look down at

America—its vastness resembling a huge mountain. I felt as if I was just a pebble in the valley.

My mother will be on the next plane, I tell myself over and over again. Just like when she sends me ahead on my own by foot, or by *tap-tap*, or by motortaxi. I tell myself that this won't be any different.

Here in Detroit Metro Airport, there are no long lines to show papers and proof to uniformed people. I ease into America's free air like a tourist returning home. With every step I take out of the terminal, I look back, and up, and around, as if my mother will appear from out of nowhere. I search for her face in the crowd of new arrivals rushing past me—some with their eyes as weary as mine, others tracking every too-bright light, every movement of each person around them, peering into every corner of this too-big place. But none of them is Manman.

I spot a lady official who is wearing the same uniform as the ones who took my mother away. I take several long steps toward her, dragging the carry-on behind me. My shoulder is sore. "Excuse me, miss? I am looking for Valerie Toussaint coming from New York," I say with my very best English.

"I'm sorry, young lady. I have no idea who that is. And there isn't another flight coming in from New York into Detroit till the morning. If you're waiting for someone to pick you up, follow the signs that read 'baggage claim,'" she says, and starts to walk away.

I shake my head. "Valerie Toussaint in New York," I say. "They took her. They say she can't come to the United States."

"You had someone with you in New York?"

I nod.

"Is she being detained?"

I stare and blink and shake my head. I search my brain for this word, trying to find the Creole word for it, or a French one—*détenir*: to hold back, to keep from moving.

The woman places both hands on her hips. Her blue uniform shirt stretches over her big chest and two buttons look like they will pop. A small black strap on the shoulder of her shirt reads TSA. Her fancy gold badge says she's an officer and another thinner badge on the other side of her black tie says her name is Deborah Howard.

"I can't help. You've been standing here all this time and your luggage is still at baggage claim. Now, follow the signs to pick up your things. I'm sure you have family waiting for you." She speaks slowly, as if I am stupid.

I purse my lips and clench my fists. How do I tell her that I am not going to the other side without Manman? How do I say that my mother has not seen her big sister, Matant Majorie, since they were teenagers and Manman wanted nothing more than to hold her face and plant a big wet kiss on her cheek? But the English words don't come as fast as the many Creole insults at the tip of my tongue for this Deborah Howard.

4

"All right. Then I will personally escort you to baggage claim," Deborah Howard says.

"No," I say. "I have to be with Valerie Toussaint."

Deborah Howard steps closer to me. At first she smells of her freshly ironed uniform, but then I smell the faint scent of cigarettes and oily food lingering behind her starchy presence. "Look. Just come back with a relative in the morning to straighten all this out. Do you understand what I just said?"

I don't make a move and I hold this moment for a little bit. Then I nod. "I understand," I say. My English is not as smooth. "I will come back."

Our four big suitcases stand alone between two luggage carousels like orphaned children. I want to ask Deborah Howard what Manman will use to brush her teeth and wash her face tonight. But I'm afraid if I give her anything to take to my mother, she will keep it and sell it at the market—if Detroit is anything like Port-au-Prince. Officer Howard grabs a nearby cart and a man helps her lift up the suitcases. I rush toward them to make sure that they don't take anything.

Night is a starlit blanket outside, and the cold air reaches my bones. I have on a long-sleeved shirt and it is not enough.

"Hope somebody's bringing you a coat," the man says, and leaves the cart right there on the sidewalk as I hug myself and rub my arms. I watch the cars pass by.

I look around and then stretch out my arms on each side

of me. I pray that Manman will get to taste this cold, free air before she rests her eyes tonight, wherever they are keeping her. And then tomorrow, she will come to this side of the glass, where there is good work that will make her hold her head up with dignity, where she will be proud to send me to school for free, and where we will build a good, brand-new life. *Une belle vie*, as she always promises, hoping that here she would be free to take her sister's hand and touch the moon.

TWO

THE COLD THREATENS to swallow me whole. Manman said that cold air is better for our skin. It will keep us fresh and youthful. In Haiti, we used to travel to the top of the mountain ranges near Au Cap for their cool winds. But here, I will turn into a block of ice.

America is more colorful than I imagined. The people are a mix of white and not-white. If only Detroit had a bunch of *blan*, it would be easier for me to pick out a single black woman and three teenage girls, but many of the women look like my aunt with their brown faces; black, shiny straightened hair; and their big, dark coats that hide their shapely figures.

I search the faces of all the people passing me and think of my cousins—the oldest, Chantal, and the twins, Primadonna and Princess, who are my age. And my aunt Marjorie. I have not seen them since I was a baby. How will they recognize me?

I am so hungry and tired. I want a container of hot, sizzling *fritay* from the streets of Delmas, my mother's warm, thick arm in mine, and her strong shoulder so I can rest my head.

A girl steps in front of me as I fidget with one of the suitcases. She lifts up her phone to my face.

"Hold up, I'm trying to see if you look like somebody," she says.

I can only tell she's a girl by the shape of her body—but her oversized jacket, loose jeans, high-top sneakers, and hat with three bumblebees on it make her almost look like a boy. I examine her round face, her deep-set eyes, and her cheeks. "Princess!" I say.

"Yep. That's you. Dang! Where you been all this time?" Princess turns and calls behind her, "Yo, I found her! She's over here!"

I reach to kiss her on the cheek and give her a big hug, but she steps back.

"Nah, I'm good, cuzz. Where's your moms?"

Another girl runs toward us—Chantal. She's smaller than Princess, with black-framed glasses—almost twenty years old. Primadonna is behind her—tall with long, flowing hair reaching down to her elbows. She's wearing sunglasses even though it's nighttime.

"Fabiola!" Chantal calls.

I reach to hug her because she's my favorite. Chantal is the one who posts links to articles and sends me messages on Facebook. She's the one who told her friends how excited she was about her cousin coming from Haiti.

"Where's Aunt Val?" Chantal asks, looking around and behind me.

I shake my head, unsure of what to say. What if they are mad that my mother didn't make it through? What if they tell my aunt and she is even angrier?

Primadonna moves closer to me, and I look her up and down to see that she is much taller because of her fancy high heels. She lives up to her name with her diva hair and sunglasses at night.

"Hi, Fabiola," she sings. Her voice is like a billion tiny bells. "So good to finally meet you. Call me Donna."

Princess steps in front of me. "And I'm Pri. Not *Princess*. Just Pri. And big sis over here is Chant."

Princess and Primadonna, or Pri and Donna now—my twin cousins. *Les Marassa Jumeaux*, who are as different as hot pepper and honey. Their faces are mirrors of each other, but their bodies are opposites—one tall and skinny and the other short and chunky—as if Princess ruled their mother's womb and Primadonna was an underfed peasant.

Chantal pushes up her eyeglasses and looks over at the baggage claim. "It's fine if you call me Chantal. So where *is* your mom?"

I turn back toward the busyness of the airport. I wonder if my mother is waiting for her flight to Detroit and praying that I don't worry about her. I wonder if she is still arguing with those uniformed people and if she has thrown those important documents in their faces and cursed their children's children. Manman will not go quietly. She will fight with her claws to get to me. "She's not here yet" is all I say.

"How long do we have to wait for her? We didn't pay for parking," Chantal says. I feel like she's looking straight through me.

"Well." I pause. "They said she's being detained in New York."

"Detained? What? She wasn't on the plane with you?" Donna asks.

My face goes hot. "From Haiti, yes. But when we got to Customs," I start to say, but my voice cracks. "They took her into a room. But maybe she will be on the next plane?"

"Shit! We thought that might happen," Pri says.

"Shut up, Pri. Don't scare her," Donna says. She pulls Pri aside and takes out her cell phone. "I'm calling Ma."

Chantal shakes her head, then turns to me. "This doesn't sound right, Fabiola," she says as she grabs my hand and pulls me back inside. We wait in line for a long time at the Delta Air Lines counter before finally reaching the man at the desk. "Hello, sir? We're looking for a passenger who might be on the next flight from New York."

Chantal's English is like that of the newspeople on TV. Her voice is high and soft, and every sentence sounds like a question, even when she gives them my name and my mother's name. It's as if she isn't sure of anything and this uniformed man behind the desk and the computer will have all the answers in the universe.

I spell out Manman's name for Chantal, who then spells it out for the man behind the counter. He prints Chantal a piece of paper and she steps off to the side. I follow her as she starts searching her phone for answers.

"What's your mother's birthday?"

I tell her. Then she asks if my mother has a middle name. I tell her that, too. She shakes her head. Chantal shows me her phone.

My mother's name is on the screen. All the other words and numbers I don't understand.

"Fabiola, your mother's going to be sent to an immigration detention center in New Jersey. She's not coming to Detroit," Chantal says. She pauses and the corners of her mouth turn down. "They're planning on sending her back to Haiti."

I can see Pri and Donna watching me from a few feet away. Donna has hung up the phone. Her brows are furrowed and she bites her bottom lip. The same look is on Pri's face.

I am quiet. Then I say, "What?"

She repeats what she said, but I only hear *sending her back to Haiti* over and over again.

If there were no blood vessels, no rib cage, no muscles holding up my heart to where it beats in my chest, it would've fallen out onto the floor.

I set my mother's carry-on down on the floor. "If New Jersey is still in the United States, then we can go get her. We can explain everything and show them that her papers are good," I say. My voice trembles.

Chantal shakes her head and puts her hand on my shoulder. "I don't know if that's how it works, Fabiola."

Chantal steps away from me and talks to her sisters with her arms crossed. Her face looks as if she is carrying the weight of all our problems on her head. We make eye contact and she smiles a little. She comes over and takes my hand. "Come on, cuzz. Let's go home."

I don't move.

I remember all those times in Port-au-Prince, standing in the open market or at an intersection waiting for my mother as the sun went down and it started to get dark and she still didn't arrive. Even as the busy streets of Delmas began to empty out and no one but *vagabon* and MINUSTAH troops passed by on motorbikes and trucks, I waited.

And she always came. She's never left me alone.

"Donna just spoke to Ma. She wants us to bring you home."

She tugs at my arm, but still, I don't move.

"Fabiola, my mother is gonna handle it, all right? She's the one who sent for you both in the first place. She'll make a few

phone calls, and before you know it, your mom will be here."
Chantal's voice is candy—sweet but firm.

She takes off her thick, long scarf and wraps it around my
shoulders—a gesture that only my mother has ever done for
me. Back in Haiti, it was always just me and Manman. But
now, my world has ballooned and in it are these three cousins,
and my aunt, too. Family takes care of each other, I tell myself.
We will get my manman.

We leave the airport. It feels like I'm leaving part of me
behind—a leg, an arm. My whole heart.

THREE

DARKNESS SEEPS INTO every crack and corner of this Detroit. Even with a few lampposts dotting the streets, I can't see the breadth and depth of this city that is my birthplace, that is now my home. I squint to see if the big mansions I've seen on American TV will glow or sparkle in the dark. I hope to catch a glimpse of the very tops of the tall buildings, but the car is moving too fast—with its fancy seats, too-loud music, and the scent of shiny new things.

Chantal sits so close to the steering wheel, her small body enveloped by the leather seat, her hands steady. Donna sits in the passenger seat and she keeps checking her reflection in the rearview mirror, the sun visor mirror, and her phone. She pulls out a big brush from her bag and brushes the ends of her long hair. Pri is next to me in the back and turns on her phone to stare at the screen. Everything is quiet, tense, until Chantal changes the music and turns the volume up really loud. The car sways a little because Pri starts to dance as she says, "Aww shit! Yo, turn that shit up some more, Chant!"

The bass reaches my insides, but it's not enough to shake the thought of my mother from my mind. I lean my forehead against the backseat window and try to see past the speeding dark and into this new world called Detroit. I try to take it all in, even the heavy music, so I can save every bit for my mother. I remind myself to smile, because finally I am here on this side of the good life.

We pull onto a smaller street and park at the corner. Chantal turns the music off and the car is still. I stare out the window. There are no mansions or big buildings here. The small houses are so close together, they might as well be holding hands.

Donna helps me out of the car. "Welcome home, Fabiola!" she sings.

The front door to a small white house swings open. There are a few steps and a narrow porch leading up to that door. I want nothing more than to rush in to let the house's warmth wrap around my cold body. A dimly lit lamp shines a light on the person standing at the door, and I recognize the face. It's like Manman's, but rounder and thicker. They have the same deep-set eyes, the same thick eyebrows that will never go away, no matter how many times they wax or pluck them. But she doesn't smile like my mother always does. Half her face barely moves, frozen from her stroke. Manman was supposed to be here taking care of that face.

She is fatter than Manman, but her clothes are smaller and tighter and shorter. Wait till my mother sees her big sister dressed like a teenager at a Sweet Micky concert, oh!

Matant Jo last saw me in person when I was a tiny baby, and since then only through Facebook photos. My aunt comes toward me, arms extended wide. She hugs me tight and I breathe in her smell. My mother has been the only family I've known my whole life, and here, in my aunt's arms, my world feels bigger, warmer.

When Matant Jo lets go, she says, "Valerie was supposed to be here. So what happened, eh?" I recognize her deep voice from all those long-distance phone calls with the 313 number. Manman said that Matant Jo used to have the sweetest bird-song voice—so sweet that she could make a man fall in love with her just by offering him a glass of water.

"Matant, they said they are detaining her," I say.

"They're sending her to New Jersey. They're not gonna let her in," Chantal adds as she takes off her boots by the door.

"But she's already in," Donna says. She sits on the arm of the living-room couch and slides off her coat. "Why would they send her to a whole other state just to send her back to Haiti, Ma?"

"Yeah, Ma, that's fucked up." Pri drags my bags to the

bottom of the stairs, then lifts one onto the first few steps. "So trying to come to America from the wrong country is a crime?"

My aunt looks at my four big suitcases and her face falls. Then she inhales deep and only one shoulder raises up to meet her breath. She shakes her head as if she's already given up.

"I will try, but . . . ," she starts to say. "These things, Fabiola . . . they are so complicated, yes?"

"*Matant Jo, n'ap jwen yon fason*," I say in Creole. "We will find a way."

"English, please." She stops to stare at me. "I hope your mother really sent you to that English-speaking school I paid all that money for."

"Yes, and I had one more year to graduate. Thank you."

"Good. Leave your mother to me. In the meantime, you will finish your junior year with Pri and Donna, okay?" she says. A bit of Haiti is peppered in her English words—the accent has not completely disappeared.

"*Wi, Matant.*"

"English!" she yells, and I jump.

"Yes, Aunt."

Pri laughs while coming back down the stairs. "Ma, don't be so hard on her. You finally got the little good girl you prayed for. She looks like she's on that straight and narrow."

"I thought I was your good girl?" Chantal whines.

"You?" Matant Jo laughs. "You were my only hope. You

17

think it was my dream for you to end up at community college? All those good grades? That big SAT score, and Wayne County Community College is all you have to show for it?"

"Here we go again," Pri mumbles as she comes to stand next to me.

Chantal sighs. "Who would've been driving you around, Ma, if I went away to college? Who would've been looking out for Pri and Donna if I left?" she says.

Chantal looks smaller without her coat. Her frame is more like mine, with her broad chest and thin legs. Everything she's said sounds like she has a good head on her shoulders. I decide then and there that we will be the second set of twins in this family. I will pay attention to what she does and how she talks. She smiles when she sees me staring at her.

Matant Jo sucks her teeth long and hard. She pulls me toward her and removes Chantal's scarf from around my shoulders. "Don't concern yourself with my crazy daughters. Come on, girl. You must be hungry."

"*Wi, Matant*," I say again, but try to swallow my words. It's habit. She's never said anything to me over the phone about speaking only in English.

"You are going to have to pay me each time you speak a word of Creole in this house."

"Yes, Matant."

"Aunt Jo. Say it just like that. Let the words slide out and don't be so uptight about it. It's just English, not too complicated."

I follow her into the kitchen as my cousins settle on the couches and someone turns on the big TV. The living room of this house, my new home, is a sea of beige leather. The furniture crowds the small space as if every inch of it is meant for sitting. I've seen bigger salons in the mansions atop the hills of Petionville, even fancier furniture and wider flat-screen TVs. But none of that belonged to me and my mother; none of the owners were family. Here, I can sit on the leather couches for as long as I want and watch all the movies in the world as if I'm at the cinema.

My aunt uses a cane to get from the living room to a narrow archway leading to the kitchen. The cabinets are a nice cherry-red color; the refrigerator and stove are a shiny silver, like the moonlight. The green numbers on the stove say it's now ten thirty at night. Matant Jo opens a cabinet, pulls out several small bottles of pills, puts them into the pocket of her short dress. The left side of her body droops and her dress slides off her shoulder.

"Are you feeling okay, Aunt?" I ask, making my voice as small as the eye of a needle.

She sighs and tries her best to stand upright. "Here they call it a stroke, but your mother would've said that the Gédé were pulling me into Ginen. Death owns half of me, Fabiola."

"Don't say that, Matant. I mean, Aunt."

"It's true. I'm sure your mother has taught you some things over the years, right? So, here is the fridge, the stove, some pots and pans. Make yourself at home. This is the house your uncle Phillip bought with his hard-earned money. This is the house your cousins were raised in. And now, I am so happy to share it with you."

She doesn't smile when she says this, and her words are as dry as cassava bread. Those words were meant for my mother, not for me. I pull out a seat from the table. But my aunt doesn't join me. She yawns, scratches her head, rubs her left shoulder, rolls her neck, and disappears into another room right next to the kitchen. I wait for her to come back, but she doesn't.

My cousins are laughing and talking among themselves in the living room. Again, there is loud music, but it comes from the TV. I don't want to be a burden to them, but I have no idea what to do in this kitchen. Suddenly, I feel so alone in this house. I am surrounded by family, but none of them really knows me or understands what happened to me today. My heart begins to ache for my mother. How could my aunt just leave me here in the kitchen—is this how you treat family in America? There is no celebration for my arrival, no meal is cooked, no neighbors are invited to welcome me, not even a glass of cool water is on the table for me to drink after such a long trip.

If my mother were here, she would quickly start gathering ingredients to make me a meal, to make everyone a meal.

I open the fridge to find bottles of soda and ketchup and hot sauce and mayonnaise and bread and eggs and too many plastic containers. In the freezer are boxes of pizza and waffles and frozen meat wrapped in plastic. My stomach is so empty, it's touching my back now. I grab a slice of orange cheese wrapped in plastic.

I jump as Pri comes into the kitchen. She's changed into what looks like her sleep clothes—a too-big T-shirt and sweat-pants.

"Come upstairs, Fabiola," she says, motioning for me to fol-low her. She's holding my mother's carry-on that I'd left by the front door. "Big day tomorrow—high school! In America! I hope you been practicing your mean mug in case you run up into some east side girls. And make sure you look 'em dead in the eye, 'cause you reppin' the west side now. Don't show weak-ness, a'ight, cuzz?"

My stomach twists at the thought of one more new experi-ence. As I follow her, I stuff the slice of cheese into my mouth, and I can't believe that this is the very first thing I eat in America. It tastes like a mix of glue, chalk, and salt.

Chantal greets me at the top of the stairs as Pri sets down the bag and goes into a small bedroom. Three doors line a narrow hallway, and Chantal points to one of them. "We're sharing a room. I don't mind." She motions toward Pri's closed door with a poster of a crown and scepter crossing each other. "That's the twins' room."

She points to another closed door. "And that's the bathroom. Now listen." She turns to face me. Her glasses are at the tip of her nose and she looks up at me over the rim. "You gotta be really smart and fast about how you use this bathroom, okay?"

I nod.

"Donna is in there now, and if you gotta pee and she's putting on her makeup or her wigs or whatever, you have to move to plan B. She locks the door and takes hours with her fake face and her fake hair. Ma probably won't let you use her bathroom downstairs. She used to beat our asses for fighting over the bathroom, and she banned us from using hers, especially after she got that Jacuzzi put in. Have you ever been in a Jacuzzi?"

I scan my memory for the English word *Jacuzzi*.

"Wait a minute. In Haiti, were you using a bathroom that's inside the house, or outside the house?"

I bite my lip trying to figure out which story to tell her. "Both, depending on whether or not there was electricity," I say. "It's complicated."

"Complicated? What's so complicated about toilets? That's a basic necessity. Ma told us how she grew up squatting over the . . . what do you call those? Latrines. Yeah. The latrines were always in the back of the house. You mean to tell me y'all still have latrines?"

A loud bang comes from Pri and Donna's bedroom and makes us jump.

"Would you two please stop talking about shit. That's nasty. I'm trying to sleep!" Pri yells from behind the closed door.

Chantal steps over and bangs back. "We're not talking about shit; we're talking about basic human necessities!"

Donna pokes her head out from the bathroom. "You know what's nasty, Pri?" she shouts. "Not washing your ass before you go to sleep, smelling like a tuna sandwich. Don't stink up my room with your tuna sandwich ass!" She shuts the door.

"Ey, ey, ey!" Matant Jo's powerful voice booms up the stairs. "Watch your mouths! You have a guest. Go to bed!"

Everything quiets for a short moment. Then Chantal laughs. "Look at your face. You're probably, like, 'What did I just walk into?'"

I smile a little as she leads me to her bedroom. It's warm and neat, like Chantal. When she turns on the light, the first thing to greet me are the shelves and shelves of books and more books. I want to stop and hug her and give her a big kiss on the cheek. With this many books I can make this place my home. I set my mother's carry-on bag down on the soft beige carpet. An air mattress lies on the floor next to her neatly made bed, which is covered with a purple blanket and too many pillows. I wonder if my mother would've slept with her sister downstairs, and think about where she's sleeping instead tonight.

Donna comes out of the bathroom and stands in Chantal's doorway. She's still dressed, and it looks as if she's put on even more makeup.

"Donna, really? You're going out now?" Chantal says.

"Just for, like, a couple of hours. . . . Driving around, that's all."

"That's not true, Donna. He's taking you all the way out to Belle Isle, isn't he?"

"No. We're just driving around. Maybe get something to eat at a Coney Island. That's all."

"Donna, please. Don't get in Dray's car while he's racing," Chantal says.

I unzip one of my suitcases and pretend not to listen, but I can't help wonder who this Dray is. Chantal is almost begging Donna not to go out.

"Dray's not gonna be racing," Donna promises. "And he don't like me in his car when he does anyway. He says I give him bad luck."

Chantal presses her hands to her forehead as if to say that Donna is not using her head. "And you don't see that as disrespectful? He's your man, but he thinks you give him bad luck? Whatever, Donna. You already made up your mind. But I'm sick of this shit."

Donna doesn't say anything, but I can see hurt flash across her face, like a strike of lightning. It's gone in an instant, hidden behind her layers of makeup and hair. The bedroom door closes and I can barely hear her footsteps going down the stairs. The sound of a car's engine filters in through the window.

"You won't be sneaking out of the house to meet up with your shitty boyfriend, right?" Chantal asks.

I turn to her, wide-eyed. "I don't have a boyfriend."

"I didn't think so. And don't get caught up in Donna and her boyfriend's shit. 'Cause he will try to holla at you. He ain't shit."

She is talking to me and not talking to me at the same time. I only listen and don't give her any response. As she climbs into bed, I open the suitcase with my mother's clothes. I pull out one of her nightgowns to wear. Hopefully, this little bit of a connection will help ease her through to this side.

"Hey," Chantal says from her bed. "I'm sorry about your mom. I wish she was here, too. Ma was saying how she was gonna be cooking and cracking jokes. Don't worry. We'll figure everything out."

I hold on to the hope in her words.

As Chantal turns off the light, I crawl onto the air mattress. It feels like clouds beneath my body. I pray for sleep to come soon, for Manman on the other side, and for Donna, who is racing out into the night with her boyfriend.

At one thirty in the morning, my eyes are burning and my stomach cries from hunger. I have not slept well since Thursday. This past week, my friends threw me a big party in our school's yard. It had been too late for us to return home, so we all spent the night sleeping on the hard concrete classroom floors. We had so much fun joking and giggling. The next few days were spent packing and giving away extra clothes and saying no to everyone who asked me to squeeze this or that into my suitcase for a loved one in Miami or Boston or New York.

We made jokes about how to pronounce Detroit. *Deux-trois*. Two-three. And Michigan rhymes with Léogâne, the town, Mee-shee-GAN. Except Americans don't say it that way. In the dark, I practice whispering "Dee-troit" and trying to get my mouth to wrap around the word just right.

Quietly, I slide off the air mattress. I need to light a candle for my mother so she can find her way back to me, but I realize I don't have matches in my bag. I tiptoe down the dark stairs to search for some.

A small lightbulb is plugged into a socket in the kitchen. The green numbers on the stove say it's now two in the morning. I open up all the drawers until I find a lighter instead, pocketing it in my mother's nightgown.

A man's voice slices through the darkness. He's singing. It's coming from outside. I move to the living-room window and I can hear the words to his song, something about dancing in the streets. It's an old catchy tune—like an American commercial. I tug apart the heavy curtains.

Again, the singing. Louder now, more joyful.

Across the street, a single lamppost shines on an empty weed-infested lot. Sitting on what looks like an overturned plastic bucket is an old man with a hat. He throws his head back and sings the last verse to his song:

Welcome to the D!
City of the Dead.
Welcome to the D!
Oh, don't let those
Hungry ghosts wake
Your little sleepy head.

He finishes out his tune with a low, guttural hum just as the deep, pounding bass of a revved car engine overrides his voice. A white car zooms around the corner and comes to a screeching stop right in front of the house.

The singing man stands up from his bucket and braces himself to sing the chorus as loud as he can.

Welcome to the D!
Better pack your lead.
Welcome to the D!
Oh, don't let that
Greedy dope boy
Get all up in your head.

At that same moment, a man comes out of the driver's side and takes long, deliberate steps toward the corner.

"Shut the fuck up, Bad Leg!" the man shouts, loud and crisp.

He reaches the singing man, grabs the collar of the old man's dirty coat, and punches him until his body is limp. The punching man lets go and Bad Leg falls to the ground—his body like an empty potato sack.

"Mind your own fucking business, old man!" the punching man shouts. He kicks him one last time before returning to the car with his fists still clenched. I can't see his face in the dim streetlight.

I shrink away from the window. I want to unsee and unhear everything. My heart is racing and there's not enough air where I'm standing. Bad Leg is still on the ground, rolling from side to side. I've seen this before—old people in Delmas who see and say too much are often beaten up or killed by young *vagabon* who have no respect for elders, for life, or for themselves.

A second man comes out from the backseat of the car—younger, slim, and wearing a blue cap. "Yo, Dray, chill!" He runs to Bad Leg to help him up.

The punching man, Dray, calls out to his friend, "Yo, get the fuck away from him!"

But the blue-cap man ignores Dray and tries to help Bad Leg to his feet. He reaches down to pick up the cane, hands it to him, and makes sure the old man is stable before walking back to the car.

At the same moment, the passenger-side door opens, and I recognize those boots and that long coat. Donna stumbles out. Her long hair hangs over her face and she can barely stand up straight. She takes several clumsy steps toward the house and I quickly close the curtains. I let the dark living room be

28

my hiding place as the front door unlocks and Donna steps in, removes her boots, and slowly makes her way up the stairs, leaving the strong scent of alcohol behind her. Her bedroom door lightly clicks shut.

I wait a few minutes before I come out of my hiding place. I replay everything until it all blurs into a dream. I want to tell Manman what I just saw and tell her that we have to go back. This corner where Matant Jo lives is no different from some of the streets in Delmas. I need to light her candles and hope that I can reach her.

Upstairs, I find a near-empty shelf in Chantal's room, move the books aside, and start taking my mother's things out of her carry-on bag: a small statue of *La Sainte Vierge*, two tea candles, the beaded *asson* gourd, a small brass bell, a white enamel mug, a cross, and a piece of white fabric. I bring the cloth up to my face and inhale the fragrance. I washed it by hand and soaked it in Florida water before we left. It smells of Manman's magic—our *lwas*, our songs, our prayers.

I move the magic things aside to dust off the shelf with my hand. I place the cloth down first, the cross in the center, then the other items around it. I add water from the bathroom sink into the mug. I'm now only missing a potted plant for the libation. I light a candle. It hisses in the dark. Chantal turns over, but a pillow covers her face.

I call my spirit guides to bend the time and space between

where I'm standing and wherever my mother is. Maybe everything is happening for a reason. Maybe this was the wrong thing to do. Maybe we should go back. What would Manman say? I need to know.

Cher *Manman,*

For all my life, you've taught me so much about how there is power and magic in our lwas, *in our songs, and in our prayers. Now, for the first time in my life, I get to test the truth of your words. This is the first night I've spent away from you and I can't even conjure an image in my mind of where you must be.*

Remember that trip to Jacmel last year when we stayed at a friend's house and you insisted that we share a mattress made for a crib? You pulled me in close and reminded me that even with my almost-woman body, I am still your one and only baby. Both our feet hung off the edge of the mattress and touched the cool concrete floor, and we prayed that a little mouse or a big spider would not eat our toes. I'm sleeping on an air mattress now and there's plush beige carpeting underneath.

When I stared into the tiny flickering flame of the tea candle tonight, an image of you and where you are finally surfaced in my mind. You told me to trust every vision, every tingling of my skin, every ringing in my ear, every itch in my palms. They're all signs. They're all the language of the lwas.

But I've heard no whispers since the moment you were pulled away from me. How could the lwas *not have given us a sign that this would happen, Manman? Were we too blinded and distracted by the excitement? This vision of you now is the only thing I have to hold.*

I can see you. You're on a bed on top of another bed. And a thin layer of itchy fabric is barely enough to cover your body. It's your first night, but you've made some friends—two men and one woman. And they are black, black like you—black as if they've sat in the hot midday sun for most of their lives selling any- and everything they could find just to make enough money to buy a plane ticket out of that hot sun. They're from Senegal, Guinea, and Cote d'Ivoire, because they speak a broken French just like you.

Matant Jo doesn't let me speak French or Creole. When you come to this side, Manman, we will speak nothing but Creole. It will help me hold on to a piece of home.

Kenbe fem, *Manman. Hold tight.*
Fabiola

FOUR

I TURN ON the bathroom-sink faucet and let the cold water wash over my hand. In Port-au-Prince, we had a well in the front yard. By this time, I would've had to wash and rinse out the bucket from the bathroom to bring it outside and pull clean water up from the well. Then I'd have to carry it back into the house and pour the well water into the tub for my bath. I can balance a bucket on top of my head, too. But I won't let my cousins see that.

"Why'd you spin around like that with the white mug in your hands?" Chantal asks when I step back into her bedroom as she makes her bed.

"You saw that? I thought you were asleep," I say. I'm already dressed, wearing one of Donna's uniforms: a gray skirt, a plain button-down white shirt, and a navy V-neck sweater. I want to go see my mother at the detention center in New Jersey. But I'm going to school. School in America. Finally. Manman had insisted that we arrive on a weekend so that I could start school the following Monday. She didn't want me to miss a day of this real American education.

"You woke me up whispering to that statue and cross. Then I saw you take the mug and spin around. What were you doing?"

"Saluting the four directions—east, west, north, and south. It's for Papa Legba. Are we going to New Jersey after school?"

"Fabiola, I'm sorry. New Jersey's ten hours away." She pulls a thick sweater down over her head. "My mother is handling it right now, and you don't even know it. And who is Papa Legba?"

"He is the *lwa* of crossroads. When there's no way, Papa Legba will make a way. He opens doors and unlocks gates," I say. "I have to pray to him so he can help my mother come to this side."

Donna barges into the bedroom. "Chant, you got an extra pair of tights?" Her black lace bra pushes her breasts up so high that they almost touch her chin.

I search her eyes for any hint of what happened last night, but they're bright, as if she's had a good night's sleep. But I know for sure that she just about fell out of that white car.

Pri comes in behind her. "Yo, Fab? You know how to braid?"

I nod and try hard not to stare at the white fabric wrapped around Pri's chest. It presses her breasts down against her rib cage until she looks like a box. The François and Toussaint women are busty. It should force us to only straighten our backs and walk with our heads held high. But one twin wears her breasts like a trophy, while the other tries to make them disappear.

"Donna, I've never seen those clothes before. You're seriously gonna wear lace thongs and a push-up bra to school?" Chantal steps closer to her. "Did you just buy those with money that you don't have?" she says through clenched teeth.

"Chant, chill. There's plenty of money to go around—we'll make it work," Donna says, tightening the straps of her new bra.

"If she went shopping, then I'm going shopping," Pri says.

"Y'all are out of control. For real. As far as I'm concerned, there is no money. Fab needs clothes and school supplies," Chantal says, pointing to me, then at her sisters. "And you already know what's happening to the rest of it."

"Why are you the only one who gets to decide how we spend our money?" Pri whines.

"'Cause I'm *responsible*, that's why," Chantal says. "And we have a deal."

Both Pri and Donna start arguing with Chantal. They yell and put their hands in her face. Chantal does the same; she doesn't back down. I can't make out the words, their reasons or logic. All I know is that there is enough money in this house for three sisters to fight over it.

"What do you want for breakfast?" I ask, trying to stop the fight. But they don't listen to me.

Quietly, I head downstairs.

There are only eggs and sliced bread. There are no plantains and avocados to make a complete Haitian breakfast. My first meal in America is one that I make for myself and eat by myself. I wonder if this is a sign of things to come.

There are footsteps upstairs. A door slams. A toilet flushes. A faucet runs. A door slams again. Then, nothing.

After washing the dishes, I fidget with the remote in the living room. Then I hear voices and cars outside. I pull back the curtains and this little slice of Detroit opens up to me—an empty paved road and small houses with only a narrow space separating one from the other.

On the opposite corner, at the edge of the lot, is a wide and short building whose graffiti-covered wall faces our house. Above it is a sign that reads LIQUOR BEER WINE PIZZA CHECK CASHING. At the other corner is a smaller building with a sign that reads HOUSE OF GOD. I stare at the liquor place, then the God place, and back.

I see the signpost at the corner, right in front of our house: American Street and Joy Road.

At the other end of the block is a house that has wooden slats for windows. It reminds me of the abandoned new houses in Port-au-Prince, where the owner had enough money to build them but not enough money to put in windows and doors. It looks like a tomb made for *djab*—angry spirits that haunt the night.

Farther to the right are vacant spaces where houses should be. They make gaping holes on the block, like missing teeth.

A few more cars start to drive down the block. The world here is awake. Manman is awake, too, for sure.

Finally, someone comes down the stairs. Pri. "Can you please braid my hair?" she asks, wearing a pair of baggy khaki pants. Her white shirt is buttoned all the way up to her neck and hangs loose over her shoulders.

I sit on the couch and she sits on a floor pillow in front of me while the news is on the TV. Donna walks by with her hair even longer than before. Her lips are redder and her eyelashes are longer, too. I contemplate asking to switch uniform skirts with her since hers is too short and mine is so long. "Is she going to a club after school?" I ask Pri.

"No. She just dresses like a ho. And I'm the only one who can call her that, you hear?"

I nod but she can't see me.

Chantal comes down the stairs while looking at her phone. "Y'all got ten minutes, 'cause first class is at eight. Whoever's not done, I'm leaving behind. Fabiola gets a pass 'cause I have to get her registered. But the two of you are just gonna have to take the bus."

"For real, Chant?" Pri says. "You gonna make your little sisters take the Livernois bus when that new ride is supposed to be for everybody? And by the time that shitty bus comes, school will be over."

"If y'all don't hurry up!" Chantal calls back.

I wonder how Matant Jo gets to work since Chantal's car is the only car I've seen parked in front of the house. So I ask, "When is Aunt Jo going to work?"

"Work?" they both say together.

"Ma is working right now," Pri says.

"Yep. She's *working* on getting your mother out of that detention center," Chantal adds. "And she certainly *worked* to get you over here from Haiti, didn't she?"

I nod again and promise myself not to ask about Matant Jo's *work* again, unless it is the work of getting my mother home.

Pri pulls away from me when I'm done braiding her hair. She stands up to check it out in a nearby mirror. "Nah. Do that shit over again. I just need six regular braids going back," she says, taking out the two I braided on each side of her head.

"But they look nice," I say.

"Don't make them look nice—just make them look . . . regular."

She comes back to sit on the floor in front of me.

"I hope y'all are ready," Chantal calls out.

"We are going to be late if I braid your hair again," I say.

"Just hurry up. Don't make them all puffy. I need them tight."

Donna examines Princess's braids from afar. "In other words, she needs them to look like a dude's," she says.

"Shut up, D," Pri says.

"Is that true? Make them look like a boy's?" I ask.

"Just make them tight, Fabiola, and hurry up."

"Why do you want to look like a boy?" I start by pulling the soft hairs at her scalp very tight.

"Are you serious right now? I'm not trying to look like nobody but Pri. Feel me?"

I glance down at her khaki pants. "You don't have to wear a uniform skirt to school like me and Donna?"

"It's cold as fuck outside. If y'all wanna wear them short-ass skirts, then that's on y'all," she says.

Pri's mouth is so dirty. Since my mother isn't here, I want to grab her little lips and twist them myself. I take my time with each braid even though Chantal has come down and is ready to leave. I want Pri to like them. I need her to like me. I'm happy to have been helpful after being here for only a few hours.

Pri leans her head on my knee and it feels like I've been here for years instead of hours—as if I'd never left in the first place. Whenever my aunt and cousins would call Haiti, I'd imagine my life as an American—living in a house full of family, going to school, having a car and a boyfriend. I shake the memory of last night from my mind—the singing man, the punching man, the saving blue-cap man, and Donna.

"I remember when we were little, you used to be the most talkative one on the phone," I say to Pri. "You would always ask to speak to me and you would tell me all about school and your friends. Remember when you said you didn't want Donna to be your twin, you wanted me to be your twin instead, and you said you were going to take the bus to Haiti?"

"Yeah, well, I'm all grown-up now, and so are you" is all she says. Then she lifts up her head and turns toward the TV.

Chantal is by the front door and starts to put on her coat, but the noise from the TV makes her stop. She glances in our direction, and Pri slowly pulls away from me. Donna comes over to stand near the TV. Pri reaches for the remote on the carpet and turns up the volume.

"... *A seventeen year-old University Liggett High School student died last week of an alleged lethal cocktail of designer drugs. Locals are now saying there have been a string of parties over the last few months where the synthetic designer drugs were*

40

made available to partygoers as young as thirteen. Police have been in contact with members of the community and have opened an investigation."

Chantal, Donna, and Pri exchange deep, quiet stares as if aiming sharp knives at one another.

Pri inhales and rubs her chin. "The fuck? They still going with this story?" she says. "One white chick OD's and there's an *investigation*? She did that shit to herself."

"Sandra McNeil actually got *killed* last month and it didn't even make the news," Chantal says.

"Did you know that white girl, Chant?" Donna asks.

"She would've been a freshman when I was a senior. I definitely don't think we were in the same circles."

The news then shifts to a report on drug cocktails and what they do to you when you take them. I'm glued to this bit of interesting information but Chantal shuts off the TV. "We're running late. Don't pay attention to that shit, Fabiola."

"I'm not done with my hair!" Pri whines.

She wants six braids and I'm only on the second.

"Fuck it," she says, and gets up from the floor. In a few minutes we're all out of the house and in the car. Matant Jo has not come out of her room.

I'm wearing a coat that used to belong to Chantal. I can't figure out the zipper and all the buttons, but Pri helps me. She then takes off her hat, leans in closer to me, and hands me a comb. I still have to finish her braids.

"I hope you're not trying to make her your little slave," Donna says. She's in the mirror again. "Fabiola, you don't have to do what Pri says. This ain't Haiti."

"Hold up. It's on her if she wants to cook and braid hair. Ain't nobody forcing her to do shit. Right, cuzz?" Pri says.

I laugh a little. "Even in Haiti, I didn't do everything that people told me to do."

"Didn't Ma and Aunt Val work as slaves when they were in Haiti?" Pri asks.

"No, dumb-ass. No one can *work* as a slave," Chantal says.

I remember those stories from Manman, too. "*Restavec*," I say. "They were not slaves, really."

"Well, did they work?" Pri asks.

"Yes, they worked."

"Did they get paid?"

"No, but . . ."

"So they *worked* as *slaves*."

Both Chantal and Donna start arguing with Pri while laughing at the same time. This isn't like the argument about money—there are more jokes and light insults. I laugh a little, too, because this moment reminds me of being with my friends back in Haiti. I can't make a straight part in Pri's hair because she and the car are moving so much. I pull her in closer and I can feel the weight of her upper body leaning on me completely. She trusts me.

I don't get to stare out into the daytime Detroit streets as I finish braiding Pri's hair. And maybe it is the feel of my hands on her scalp that makes her open up to me, so she is the first to tell her story. With each braid, with each touch, I begin to know and understand my dear cousins, my sisters from another mother.

PRINCESS'S STORY

Ma named us Primadonna and Princess 'cause she thought being born in America to a father with a good-paying job at a car factory and a house and a bright future meant that we would be royalty. But when our father got killed, that's when shit fell apart. We don't remember too much of that 'cause we were little. But by the time we got to middle school, Ma had the newest car on the block—a minivan with leather seats. Then later, we had the first flat-screen, the first laptops, the first cell phones out of everybody we knew. Yeah, there were dudes always rolling up to the house with stacks, and other dudes standing on our front steps keeping watch and shit. But we did all right. We did better than all right.

You'd think bitches would respect us for having a mother who did whatever it takes to keep her daughters fed, dressed, and safe. But no. In the second grade, this little bitch stole my Dora the Explorer book bag. That's when I learned how to fight. Chantal got it the worst because she was actually born in Haiti and she still spoke Creole. And Ma did our hair in these big, dookie braids with rainbow barrettes and bows and shit. They thought just 'cause we were Haitian, we didn't bathe, we wore mismatched colors, and we did voodoo. The nice ones just kept asking us if we spoke French. Even though Chantal kept telling them that "Sak pase? Map boule!" is not French. It's Creole, bitch.

Donna and her fast ass was the first one to get a boyfriend, and she always liked to tell people that she was French. Like from Paris, France, for real. This one time, a crew of girls from the east side challenged Donna on her Frenchness. They jumped her, but we all know that's not why they beat her up. Donna was tall and pretty and had all the guys from here to the east side wanting to holla at her. Now, I didn't give a fuck if other girls called me fat, but I swear, anybody lay a hand on my sister . . . So, yeah. I beat the shit out of that girl. And her friends, too.

In middle school, it got around that we spoke French. And some dumb motherfucker started calling us the Frenchie Sisters. It didn't help that our last name is François. By high school, Chantal had gotten a scholarship to some fancy prep school, University Liggett, Donna was going out with Dray, and I was . . . well, let's just say

I was the brawn. I don't remember who came up with it first, but Chantal is the brains, Donna is the beauty, and me, I'm the brawn. Three Bees. The biggest, baddest bitches from the west side. Nobody, I mean nobody, fucks with us.

FIVE

"DOESN'T IT LOOK like a haunted castle?" Chantal asks after she parks the car.

I step into my very first snowfall. It started a few minutes ago while we were in the car. The roads here are so wide and straight and clean. We pass a small crowd standing near what looks like a bus stop—a tiny glass shelter with a single bench. Their hoods and thick coats make them look like the fat iguanas that cling to the bright-red flamboyant trees back home. Nothing here is alive with color like in Haiti. The sun hides behind a concrete sky. I search the landscape for yellows, oranges, pinks, or turquoises like in my beloved Port-au-Prince. But God has painted this place gray and brown. Only a thin white sheet of snow covers the burned-out houses and buildings. The flakes seem to appear from out of nowhere, like an invisible hand sprinkling salt onto zombies.

I am no zombie. I sniff the salty snow-filled air to make sure that I stay alive and human. If it's snowing in New Jersey, I hope Manman does the same. The thought that my mother may not be seeing outside crosses my mind and I shake it off.

I glance up and down the wide street before stepping into the haunted castle that will be my new school. A few cars stop in front of the building and teenagers spill out onto the sidewalk. Pri and Donna leave for their first class, while Chantal and I head to an office where students wander in and out—most with their uniform skirts shorter than mine. I pull my skirt up a bit.

"Yeah, I know it's below your knees," Chantal says. "You don't have to be like everybody else."

"Not even in Haiti do girls my age wear their skirts so long, unless they've devoted their lives to being a virgin," I say.

Chantal stares at me for a long second. Then she laughs. "Well, are you a virgin?"

Before I can answer, someone calls out Chantal's name. A white woman with orange hair comes toward us with open arms.

"Chantal François," the lady says. "Look at you."

"Hi, Ms. Stanley." Chantal's voice is as sweet as mangoes, and she smiles big and bright and holds her head down. She becomes a different Chantal, like the one at the airport.

"Liggett took what could've been our best student away. How'd they treat you over there? Lemme guess. You're up for the weekend from Yale? Harvard? Princeton?"

Chantal shakes her head and the smile disappears from her face.

"Okay. I remember you saying you wanted to get as far away from Detroit as you possibly could. Stanford? UCLA?" The lady is holding both Chantal's hands and is looking straight into her eyes.

"ULS was fine and college is great, Ms. Stanley" is all Chantal says. Then she turns to me. "This is my cousin, Fabiola. She just got here from Haiti."

This Ms. Stanley is like an overripe banana—too sweet and mushy. She's so excited about my coming from Haiti, she hugs me for too long and holds my hand too tight. She asks so many questions I can't keep up, until she finally asks if I speak English. Chantal answers for me.

"Well, great. Let's get you all registered," she says. "I'm sure you're excited to be going to school with your cousins."

We follow Ms. Stanley into her office. Chantal and I sit at a desk while the woman pulls out a folder from a file.

"You have all the documents you need?" Ms. Stanley asks.

Chantal takes out a big yellow envelope from her bag and slides it to Ms. Stanley. "My mother will come in with all her documents. We just didn't want her to miss a day of school and have to stay at home alone and all."

I quickly turn to Chantal, but she shoots me a look that says *trust me.*

Ms. Stanley takes the thick envelope without opening it and nods. "You know, those documents won't really be necessary for now. This should cover her tuition for a while. How is your mother doing, by the way?"

"She's fine," Chantal says quickly.

Ms. Stanley nods, smiles, and disappears out of the office with the envelope.

Chantal turns to me and says, "My mother worked hard to make sure that you and your mother are taken care of. And she's not just making bank—she is the damn bank. But your cousins think it's gonna last forever. I keep telling them we have to save."

"Matant Jo is a bank?" I ask with my eyes wide.

"Well." Chantal pauses. Then she inhales and says, "Yeah, you can say that. She loans money out. Makes money from the interest. Like a bank, but a whole lot less complicated, and a whole lot riskier. So yeah, like I told you this morning, she works her butt off."

I fidget with the pleats on my uniform skirt. "Why don't I go to a free school?" I ask.

"Did you go to a free school in Haiti?"

"Free school in Haiti? No way."

"All right, then. Ma thinks that anything free is just bullshit. Especially in this city. You don't want a bullshit education."

Ms. Stanley comes back in and motions for me to leave the office with her. Chantal waves me off.

"Honey, tell me how you pronounce your full name," Ms. Stanley says before we enter a loud classroom.

"Fabiola Toussaint. FAH-BYO-LA TOO-SAINT," I enunciate slowly.

With Matant Jo's money back in Haiti, my mother was able to send me to one of the very best English-speaking schools. My classmates were the sons and daughters of NGO executives, Syrian businessmen, Haitian *foutbòl* stars, and world-renowned musicians. We were all shades of brown and not-brown. This is what the tuition paid for—to be with other students who were examples of the world.

Here, the class fidgets and talks loudly and the teacher rushes his lesson.

I have no pens, no notebook, no textbook—only my ears and memory. I try to keep up, but I quickly introduce myself to the girl sitting next to me as the other students get up from their seats and leave the classroom.

"That's a pretty name," she says, tossing her long locks back.

"My mom named me," I say, then wish I'd said something more interesting.

"I'm Imani," she replies. I can't take my eyes off her hair.

"They're real. You can grow them, too, if you want. You just have to be patient. Where's that accent from?"

"Haiti," I say, trying to say it like Americans. We walk out of the classroom together.

"That's right. You the Three Bees' cousin," she says, examining me from head to toe.

I almost don't want to be the Three Bees' cousin from the way this Imani looks at me. So I start to walk quickly ahead of her.

"Wait," she says, following behind me. "Everyone thinks you're the Fourth Bee."

"Me? The Fourth Bee? No way!"

"But Pri is going around telling everybody not to mess with her cuzz. She's scaring the boys away, too, in case they might wanna holla at you," Imani says as she pulls her heavy book bag over her shoulder.

I don't let her see me smile. "They're my cousins, but I am not a . . . *bee*."

"I know you're from Haiti and all, so if you knew about the stories I've heard, you'd want to have the Three Bees as your fam. You tell anybody that Pri and 'em over on Joy Road are your cousins, you'll be like royalty."

"What stories?" I start to ask. Students pour out into the hallway and Imani moves closer to me so she can whisper.

"They just go hard for each other," she says really low. "If something goes down with Donna, Pri is right there fighting for her. And I hear she throws some hard punches. She don't fight like a bitch with all that hair pulling and scratching.

Chantal, on the other hand, uses her rich-people connects from her old high school to get people's cars towed and shit like that. And 'cause they're Haitian, everybody thinks they do that voodoo shit. Is it true? Do they put hexes on people? I hear their mother is a voodoo queen who goes by Aunt Jo."

I let out a loud laugh, because everything Imani says sounds so outrageous. Then I quickly cover my mouth because the students start looking at me. I can feel their whispers on my skin. I don't want all this attention. If my cousins are indeed royalty here, then I am just a peasant who only wants a good education, opportunity for a good future, and my mother. This is what she hopes for me, too.

I have two more classes with Imani and then it's time for lunch. I watch my cousins in the cafeteria. They fold their wild, crazy selves into tiny squares at school—no fighting, no cursing, just royal. Donna walks as if she's a supermodel—with her done-up face and her flowing hair and her nose in the air. The boys go out of their way just to say hi to her. Pri knows everyone and she's always telling jokes and laughing. At the end of the day, when Chantal picks us up, she attracts a small crowd who insist on talking to her about everything and nothing. My cousins are indeed royalty here.

Never could I have imagined being in a house full of family and still feeling lonely. Loud music plays upstairs and the TV blares downstairs. No one is cooking in the kitchen even with the nice stove and refrigerator filled with food. I'm sitting at the table eating my dinner out of paper bags—a hamburger, French fries, and soda.

The whole house seems to want to squeeze me in, force a deep wail from out of my body because it's only been one day and I am losing myself to this new place. This is the opposite of the earthquake, where things were falling apart and the ground was shifting beneath my small feet. Here, the walls, the air, the buildings, the people all seem to have already fallen. And there is nothing else left to do but to shrink and squeeze until everything has turned to dust and disappeared.

But not yet. Not without my mother.

I get up from the table and gently knock on Matant Jo's bedroom door three times before I say her name the way she wants me to say it. "Aunt Jo?"

I hear footsteps and shuffling. She opens the door. She squints her eyes, and her hair is thin and lies flat against her head. She's been wearing a wig all this time.

"My mother is still not here," I say. My voice trembles, and the words come out of my mouth like a sudden rainstorm.

"I know" is all she says at first. She shuffles to the edge of her bed. It's a little dark in the room and there's a small TV on top of a dresser. The volume is down and I wonder what she does in there all day. Then she says, "My hands are tied, Fabiola. I did everything to get my sister here. Everything. I would've kissed the ground if she had walked through that door with you."

"You knew she wasn't coming, Matant? I mean, Aunt."

"Things are complicated."

"She was on the line with me. She had all her papers. They gave her a visa."

"I know, I know," she says, holding her head down. "You are smart. Your mother told me how your English was so good that those Americans had no choice but to grant her a visa."

"It wasn't me. She had all her papers. She was supposed to be here. They were supposed to let her in."

She motions for me to come inside her bedroom. I step over some clothes and stand next to her bed.

"In some ways," she says, "this country is like Haiti. They talk out of two sides of their mouth. You can never know what these people are going to do."

"Aunt Jo, is my mother coming or not?" I ask. I know how adult Haitians can talk in riddles and never give you a straight answer. Even with her years of living in America, this is still true for my aunt.

She exhales. "Fabiola, those people and their rules are like sorcerers. If I go digging too deep into their trickery, I will end up with an ass for a face, and a face for an ass."

"You are saying no. My mother is not coming? They are sending her back?"

She doesn't answer and points to the dresser where the

small TV sits. "The fourth drawer," she says. "You will see a book, a Bible. Bring it to me."

I do as she says. She takes the Bible and pats the spot next to her on the bed. I sit beside her and feel her warm arm against mine. It almost feels like my mother's. Almost.

MATANT JO'S STORY

This is your home now, Fabiola. This is Phillip's house—the house he bought with the last bit of money he had from Haiti. He had dreams, you know. That's why when he saw this house for sale, on the corner of American Street and Joy Road, he insisted on buying it with the cash from his ransacked and burned-to-the-ground car dealership in Port-au-Prince. He thought he was buying American Joy. So he sent for me and our baby daughter, Chantal. I could not have asked for anything more—a house, a bit of money, and the love of my life. He was all I had—no friends, no family, no Haitian community like in Miami or New York. He was my everything. He came here for the cars and car factories. You'd think it would've been a car that killed him since he loved them so much. But no. The car he left behind is gone now, but we have this house. Even if everything burns to the ground by some twisted magic, it will still be the last house standing. But Phillip also left a hole in my heart, like the bullet wound in the back of his head. This hole has spread around me like a cancer. Maybe that will be my salvation, my death. Cancer, another stroke, a heart attack. Now that I won't ever see my dear sister, I don't care how I go. Maybe you, like my daughters, will fill this hole with a little bit of love until my time comes.

SIX

MATANT JO KEEPS a stash of money in her dresser, inside a Bible. She gave me a pair of one-hundred-dollar bills, two fifties, and five twenties from a pile of endless bills. She said it's for my *expenses*. I promise myself not to let the cousins know that I have this money. I don't want to join in on their arguments.

So I carry the four hundred dollars in my bag, in a wallet, as if it's simply pocket change. It's the most money I've had to myself. It makes me walk taller and speak with more confidence. This unearned cash makes me feel a little bit more American. This is the beginning of the good life, I think.

It's Friday and Chantal has come to the school early to run errands with Pri and Donna. I was told to wait in the lobby until four o'clock, a whole hour after school has ended. I wonder what it is that they need to do that shouldn't involve me. But still, I'm grateful for the little bit of freedom. And with my money, I have more courage to step out into this new free world.

There are still kids in the building practicing sports and participating in clubs, and some of them sit outside on the steps talking and laughing. As I walk outside, some say hi and some ignore me, but they still know that I'm the Three Bees' cousin, as they say. I look up and down the block—Vernor Highway. Other kids are walking to the bus stop. I have enough money to take the bus all the way to the end of Detroit and back if I want to. I can even walk into a restaurant to eat by myself or go to a store to shop for clothes.

I let my feet take me down the block to a big store called CVS pharmacy. I almost run across the intersection even though the lights say I have the right of way. I don't trust these speeding cars with too much road around them. A woman bumps into me, or I into her. I can't tell because she seems to appear from out of nowhere. I quickly apologize with my very best English and step away. Any hint of an accent could be an invitation for judgment—that I'm stupid and I don't belong here. But the woman is kind and smiles and apologizes, saying that it was her fault.

But then she asks, "Are you from around here?"

"Yes." I nod. I look down at her clothes and shoes. Her coat is decent and clean, her jeans are plain, her boots look new, and her face is hard, but safe—like a schoolteacher's. But still, she's a stranger. I start to walk away.

"Do you go to that high school over there?" she asks. "Catholic, right? I hear it's good."

I turn to her and only smile a little.

The lady follows me into the CVS, but she goes down another aisle as I stand there staring at the enormity of it all. So many things to buy. So many choices. Matant Jo was right about this country talking out of two sides of its mouth. This store is more than just a pharmacy. I walk out with only a bag of potato chips, juice, lip gloss, and gloves.

When I'm back at the school, Chantal and the twins are already waiting at the curb. As we pull away, I spot the lady who bumped into me, or I into her. I don't know. She seems to be staring at this car, right into this window. Or maybe she's looking at the school since she asked about it. I can't tell for sure. I watch her from the backseat of the car as she walks down the block alone. Pri has already dug her thick hand into my bag of potato chips. I don't ask where my cousins have been or why they left me. I'm only grateful.

Something tugs at my belly and I turn to the back window, looking for that lady again. But she's long gone now.

SEVEN

ON MY FIRST Saturday night here, music pumps through every corner of the house. The bass pulses in my bones and I wish I could plug my ears. Aunt Jo is dressed up in too-tight jeans and a nice bright shirt for the first time since I arrived, and she has guests in the living room—four men who smoke and curse just as much as Pri. If Matant Jo is a bank, then these men must be her bank tellers. Except no customers come to the house.

I avoid going downstairs even though I'm hungry. Manman will not believe me when I tell her that I am hungrier here than I ever was in Port-au-Prince. Not from a lack of food, but from a lack of willing and able cooks.

Donna has picked out my clothes for a birthday party—a new black dress that's so tight, it looks like another layer of skin.

I'm sitting on the edge of Chantal's bed, waiting for Donna to do my hair, when Pri comes in and stands right in front of my altar. She stares at the magic things for a while without touching them before she asks, "Does it work?"

"Well," I say. "Has anyone ever tried to kill you?" I have to speak loudly over the music.

Pri turns around and closes the bedroom door, muting the music a bit.

"Kill me? Ain't nobody rolling up in this house to kill anyone."

"I know. We made it so. Me and my mother. Every day we asked the *lwas* to protect our family in Detroit and their house," I say, adjusting my bra.

"Oh, you did some voodoo shit to protect us?" she asks with her arms crossed.

"It's not voodoo shit," I tell her. "Manman told me that ever since Uncle Phillip was killed, she had to find answers to why God took away the one true love in her sister's life. But only the *lwas* were able to give her answers. They speak to her, and she listens."

Pri comes to sit next to me on the bed. "Fabiola, I know you're family and all, but keep my father's name out your mouth," she says, and kisses two of her fingers and raises them up to the ceiling.

I nod, even though my mother has been setting up shrines and praying for Pri's father's soul on the anniversary of his death each year. And we always say his name in remembrance—Jean-Phillip François.

Donna barges into the bedroom wearing only her fancy underwear and holding a basket filled with combs, curlers, a curling iron, a flat iron, a blow-dryer, pomades, hair lotions, and makeup. "Ready for your fabulous makeover, Fabiola?"

"No," I tell her.

"Well, you need one," she says, and starts with my hair anyway.

By the time she's done, fake hair flows down my back and my new face looks plastic—my eyebrows are perfectly arched and thicker than I've ever seen them, my lips are magically fuller, and my eyelashes look like bangs for my eyes.

Pri, Aunt Jo, and her friends all cheer and clap when I come down the stairs in borrowed high heels that make my legs wobble, and Donna takes a few pictures of me. Chantal only shakes her head as if she disapproves of the whole makeover. I want to tell Donna not to put them on the internet, but maybe this new self will reach my mother and she will come to smack the makeup from off my face and rip the tight dress from my body.

Chantal drives us, but she doesn't come to the party. "Be careful, y'all! And look out for each other," she says as Pri gives her a time to pick us up.

"Why don't you come?" I ask her before getting out of the car.

"I have a big test this week" is all she says.

64

This birthday party is at a nightclub—a plain, short, and wide building. It has one narrow purple door with the letter Q on it drawn in bright-silver paint. The street is crowded with people, and a few come over to say hi and hug my cousins. My cousins' friends stare at me and start asking too many questions.

It's not their bodies inching closer that make me nervous, it's their words that sound just like the heavy bass music—hard and fast like too-loud conga drums.

The smell is different here. Not like in Port-au-Prince, where everyone on the street is a mix of sweat, gasoline, and baby powder. Here, it smells like the MINUSTAH troops who hang out at the clubs in Petionville on Saturday nights—alcohol, marijuana, and lust. Some of my friends would go for money and a good time, but I never liked it.

Pri pulls my arm hard, away from the crowd, and yells, "Y'all better not put a finger on my cousin, or it's my fucking fist in your face!"

"Yo, chill, Pri!" a guy standing nearby says. "Ain't nobody checking for your cousin."

"You better not. Nasty ass," Pri says.

The guys standing on the sidewalk are all covered with thick, dark coats and baseball caps that shield their eyes. They hold red plastic cups in one hand while the other hand is shoved into a pocket of jeans that hang too low below their waist. They are the *vagabon* who Manman tells me to stay away from because they lead to nothing but trouble, the *vagabon* who my friends like to have as boyfriends because they can rap and have their own money and cars. Wyclef is their god and American rap videos are their church. But those Port-au-Prince *vagabon* are fakers. These Detroit *vagabon* are the real thing.

As Pri pulls me in through the purple door, my eyes lock with one of the *vagabon*. He pushes his blue cap up and stares right at me, smiling. I stare back at him until I recognize him. The blue-cap boy—the one who came out of the car to help Bad Leg. He's not a man but a boy, probably my age. I smile a little, too—my small way of saying "thank you."

Inside is as dark as it is outside. Bodies are pressed up against one another just like they do on the narrow, crumbled sidewalks of Delmas. The men are in their coats while most of the women are dressed like in the American music videos—short, shiny dresses that look like tinfoil around their thighs, shoes with heels like ice picks, and hair from the tails of horses. Here, there is more smoke, more alcohol, and the conga drum voices blend with the heavy bass music. Pri has to push her way through. Some people stop to give her a hug. Some smile at me and tell me, "Welcome to the D, shorty!"

Someone hands me a red plastic cup and I take it because I'm thirsty and hungry. But it's alcohol. Not Prestige beer or Rhum Barbancourt—the strong, bitter, or sweet alcohol made for men who talk politics and play dominoes into all hours of the night. Pri has a red plastic cup, too, and she pours the alcohol down her throat as if it's cool water on a hot day.

The music changes. It's faster now, and I look back at the crowd. Everyone dips and sways to the rhythm. It's the familiar music my friends like, too. But they don't dance the same way. Here, everyone knows the words; everyone dances to the beat just right.

A guy wearing an eye patch steps closer to me and starts dancing. His presence feels like a heavy shadow, a darkness. Then Pri puts both her hands on his chest and pushes him away from me. He laughs, then tries to give her a hug.

As he talks to Pri, something about the way he stands and moves triggers a memory. If the blue-cap boy is outside the club, then the punching man is standing right in front of me. I'm sure of it because he has the same stance, the same gait. The blue-cap boy called him Dray.

When I get a better look at his face, my stomach sinks. He's definitely the one who punched Bad Leg. He looks younger up close, but older than me—maybe Chantal's age. There is a black patch over his left eye and his face is a series of sharp lines—a tight jaw, a straight nose, and a hard smile. Even if I hadn't seen him do that to the poor old man, something about the way he grins and that eye patch makes him look like he's been to the underworld and back.

I've learned to recognize these faces back in Port-au-Prince.

There are harmless *vagabon* who are just as scared as you are when they try to steal your money at knifepoint; and then there are the *malfekté*, the truly evil, who are not afraid to stick that knife into your belly. He is *malfekté*, for sure.

"I'm just fucking with her. You can't keep her in a cage while she's here, Pri," Dray says. His voice sounds as if it's coming from the depths of dark, broken places. I can feel it in my bones.

"I don't like all these guys staring at her like she's fresh meat," Pri replies.

"She is fresh meat. And I'm sure she can take care of herself. Haiti's rougher than the D and Chi-Town put together." He licks his lips while staring at me with his one good eye.

"I can take care of myself," I say. Maybe too loud.

The man laughs. "Of course you can take care of yourself," he says. "You're gonna have to. And your English is pretty good, shorty. I'm Dray, by the way." He holds out his hand for me to shake. It's cold and rough. He squeezes my hand and it's as if he's sent shards of glass down my body. I pull away. He shrugs and smiles his fake smile as Donna and another boy come over to us—the blue-cap boy. Dray slaps the boy's hand and then slides his arm around Donna's waist, squeezing her butt—as if he owns these two people.

"This is my cousin, Fabiola," Donna says to the blue-cap boy.

"Fab what?" he asks, easing closer to me.

I step back. "Fabiola."

"Fabulous?" he asks.

"Fabiola!" both Pri and I shout.

"Fabulous," he says.

"No. FAH-B-YO-LAH!" I shout over the music.

"FA-BYOU-LESS," he says even louder. "I'm Kasim. KAH-SEEM."

I laugh because his name sounds like the Creole word for "break me." So I say, "Broke."

"What? Broke?"

"If you call me Fabulous, I will call you Broke."

He laughs. "You got jokes? I'm far from being broke, sweetheart." He steps closer to me.

I step away again. "Broke," I repeat.

"Fabulous," he says again, licking his lips while he grabs my hand.

"Let go of me, Broke," I say, pulling away from him.

He lets go. "You got some fire in you, Fabulous."

I roll my eyes and turn away. If he has anything to do with Dray, then I don't want anything to do him. I don't need a *vagabon*'s attention right now. I'm still wearing my coat even though everyone has taken theirs off and it's as hot as Haiti in here. My dress is too tight and too short and I don't want Dray's piercing eyes on me, not even the blue-cap boy's, Kasim. So I pull up the thick collar and cross my arms. I even begin to wish Chantal was here—at least there would be someone to sit next to me. But she has to study. I want to study, too, so I promise myself to stay behind with Chantal the next time my wild twin cousins decide to go to a party.

Pri and Donna seem to know the whole world here. Donna does all the talking, and Pri dances while a small crowd begins to form around her. She moves her feet about so fast, she looks as if she's tap-dancing. She dips and kicks and spins on her toes and crouches down to the floor with one leg behind her other leg. I have to stand up now to see her. A boy comes into the circle and does the same thing Pri is doing, except with stronger kicks and faster spins.

I finally take my coat off and hang it over the chair, so I can try to do one of those moves. But I almost break an ankle. Someone next to me laughs. I turn to see Kasim leaning against a nearby wall. I roll my eyes and let out a long, tired sigh.

"You're trying to do the Detroit Jit, Fabulous? I can show you," he says, and starts to walk over to me.

He does something funny with his feet and pretends to trip. I turn away to hide my smile.

"Hey! I saw that smile. Finally!"

I shake my head and put on a serious face again.

"Are all Haitian girls built like you?"

"What? Built like me?"

"I mean, you know, strong and Ford tough."

I shake my head and walk away from him. He gasps.

"Damn, shorty! That dress!"

I keep walking and pushing my way through the crowd.

He follows me and I stop when I see Donna and Dray in a corner at the other end of the club. He has his arm around her neck and her head is pressed up against his pit where all his sweat rubs against the top of her hair. It looks like he is choking her.

"Why is your friend doing that to my cousin?" I ask Kasim, pointing with my chin.

"Who? Dray and Donna? We call them D&D. Dungeons and Dragons. He's the dungeon and she's the dragon. Dray is putting her in a headlock to tame that dragon."

"What? Donna? A dragon?"

"I guess you don't know your cousins very well," Kasim says. He moves closer to me as Pri's circle disperses and people start to crowd back onto the dance floor. "Don't worry. We won't be like them. You'll just be your Fabulous self, and I'll keep being Broke Kasim. We could be Fabulous and Broke."

I laugh and cover my mouth, and he pulls my hand away. I let him see me smile. "Your name . . . it means 'broke' in Creole."

He smiles back and he keeps holding my hand. "Oh, really? I can't have that. Then call me 'filthy rich' in Creole instead." He licks his lips. "You look real nice in that dress, though."

A song I know comes on and my body obeys the familiar rhythm. We dance, but I don't dare look into his face. Instead, I keep my eyes on Donna as Dray gives her a drink. A slower song comes on—not one that will force me to lay my head on Kasim's shoulder, but one that makes him pull me in at the waist and press my body against his. I push him away because my heart is beating too fast. I look around as if my mother's eyes are in the walls here. But it's Pri who is staring at us. She doesn't smile or nod in approval. She simply watches Kasim. Kasim follows my gaze and laughs.

"You gonna let your cousin cock block?" he asks with his dimpled smile.

I step away from him. "Cock block? Excuse me, but there will be no *cock* over here, okay!"

I leave him to his cock and walk back to my seat next to the food. Pri laughs from afar as Broke Kasim stands there with his mouth open, catching flies, as Manman would say. I don't move even as everyone surrounds the birthday girl to wish her a happy eighteenth.

The night goes on and Kasim is always a few feet away, watching my every move while talking to friends and even other girls. I watch him, too, from the corner of my eye. Even though I told him to get away from me, there is something pulling me closer to him. I lose track of my cousins and realize the room is almost empty.

"They're already outside," Kasim says, coming over to me with my coat.

Outside, I spot Pri in front of the club, yelling at Dray.

Donna is a few feet away, crouched down with her hair hanging to the ground.

I run to help. I pull her hair back and check her forehead. "Donna? What's wrong?"

"Here. Give her some water." Kasim holds out a plastic cup as I try to get Donna to sit up.

"She should've left your ass a long time ago!" Pri shouts, and her voice echoes down the dark street. Most of the partygoers are still in front of the club even though it's like a refrigerator out here. Everybody stares at us, but no one seems to care that Donna is sick.

A small group of adults comes over and starts to ease us away from the building.

"Donna," Dray says, trying to make her stand up. "I'll take you home."

"Hell no, you ain't taking her home!" Pri shouts.

"I wanna go with him," Donna mumbles. She holds her head up and finally opens her eyes to take Dray's arm, but she still stumbles forward on the sidewalk.

"See? That's what I'm talking about, D," Pri says. "You like the way he treats you? You're not going into the car with him, Donna! He kept giving you drinks when you were about to pass out."

"She asked for them!" Dray says, yanking open the passenger door of his white car.

Donna drops her body into the seat.

"She's getting real tired of y'all trying to control her life," Dray says as he slams the car door. "Pri, just 'cause y'all twins don't mean y'all joined at the motherfuckin' hips."

Pri inhales and clenches her fists. She bangs on the hood of a nearby car.

At the same moment, I notice Chantal's car pulling up to the curb. She quickly comes over to Dray's car. "What's going on?" she yells. Her voice is different again, harder, as if she's had to do this plenty of times before.

"Calm the fuck down, Chantal. I'm gonna take her home," Dray says. "I don't need to be dealing with this shit."

"I'll ride in the back," Kasim says as he goes over to Dray's car.

As if the boy already has my heart tied to his littlest finger, I say, "I'll go, too. I will make sure she's okay."

I don't even glance at my cousins to see if they would stop me. In the blink of an eye, I'm in the warm backseat of Dray's car with Kasim next to me. It smells like a mix of freshly chopped wood and wild leaves—marijuana. I cover my nose and keep my eyes on my cousin, even as Kasim keeps looking over at me, smiling, and inching his hand closer and closer to my leg.

When we reach Aunt Jo's house, Chantal and Pri are already standing in front, and the car is parked at the curb. The singing man is on the corner again. I can't make out the words to his song, but I lean toward Dray in the driver's seat. "Don't hit him again," I say.

He turns to me and so does Donna. "Who? Bad Leg? Nobody gives a fuck about him."

Just as he says this, Bad Leg's voice reaches my bones—it's as smooth as a river, and it ebbs and flows and ripples at just the right moments. I can't pull away from his song as I get out of that car. Pri has come over to help Donna, and she curses Dray one last time.

As we all enter the house and Dray and Kasim zoom off into the night, Bad Leg finishes his song with these words:

> *Love me to the moon and back.*
> *Come on, babe, just cut me some slack.*
> *Baby, why you always on the attack?*
> *Put up your dukes, ha!*
> *Show me them nukes, yeah!*
> *And launch me to the moon and back.*

Cher *Manman,*

*I see you clearer now because I light my candle and pour
the libation, rattle the* asson, *and ring the bell to call all
my guides, the* lwas. *You've told me that they are here for
me. All I have to do is call on them so they can help me. I
believe you, Manman. Even without you being here to
hold ceremonies with drummers and singers and a village of
followers, I will practice all that you've taught me.*

*There, within the flame of the tea candle again, you
are on your bed crying into a piece of brown paper. It's too
rough on your cheeks and nose, so you use the white sheet
instead. You're careful not to let anyone see you cry. How
did you get there, Manman? What did you do? Is it because
you are a* mambo—*a Vodou priestess who held ceremonies
in the courtyard of a Christian NGO building? Are they
punishing you for that, Manman? Are they punishing me?
I've searched my memory for all the sinful things I've done.
I let Marco touch me the night before we left. Was the* lwa
*of love and fertility, Ezili, mad at me for that? Is that why
she summoned her lover, Papa Legba, to block you from*

entering the gates to this freedom, to this sister of yours, to
your nieces, and to me?

Matant Jo misses you so much that she is incapable of
doing anything for herself. The other day, she held my face in
her hands and prayed to God that it was your face and not
mine. And just like I saw you do in the tea-candle flame,
she grabbed the corner of her white sheet and wiped her
tears.

Kenbe fem. *Hold tight.*
Fabiola

EIGHT

"**DOES DRAY HIT** her?" I ask Chantal and Pri after Donna is all bathed, in her pajamas, and passed out. It seems like no one else wants to sleep tonight. Pri and I are playing a card game while Chantal reads.

"Why? Did you see him hit her?" Pri holds her cards up as if she makes money from these games. She shuffles and deals like a gambler.

"The singing man on the corner said so. It's like his poetry and songs are what he sees. He said something about an attack and putting up dukes. That's like hitting and fighting, right?"

"What are you talking about? Bad Leg? He actually told you that shit?"

"It was in his poem if you listened."

"Nobody listens to Bad Leg—that crazy-ass man. Some people around here even call him the devil. Got needle marks all up his arm and still ain't dead. Ma said he was a crackhead when she first moved here. He's gotten beaten up, burned up, tossed over the overpass on the highway, thrown in the river, and he still show up right there on that corner."

"Why do they call him Bad Leg?"

"I'll give you twenty dollars to ask him." Pri puts down a two of diamonds. "For every person who has ever asked Bad Leg what happened to his leg, he tells a different story each time."

"Yep." Chantal looks up from her book. "I must've asked him fifty times and he gave me fifty different stories—his leg got crushed in Iraq, it got caught in a machine at a factory, Detroit rats nibbled on it when he was homeless."

"Ain't he still homeless? And he told me he was tortured by an east side gang," Pri says as she collects my small pile of cards into her growing pile.

"I will get the real story," I say.

My cousins are all asleep, but I'm still awake, staring at the low white ceiling and counting my problems with every breath. I have not slept since being in this new home; I only rest my eyes. The events of the week play out over and over in my mind like a looping movie—my cousins' voices are the background music to the broken Detroit streets, the easy and boring teachers and schoolwork, the trips to McDonald's and pizza spots, and the endless seconds, minutes, hours without my mother. The singing man on the corner named Bag Leg provides the lyrics.

Chantal's clock says it's three thirty in the morning, and Bad Leg's voice eases through the locked windows and thick curtains to hover above my air mattress. His river-smooth song pulls me up out of bed. Chantal's window faces the front of the house, so I see Bad Leg to the far left, still sitting on the overturned plastic bucket with a streetlight shining over him like a limelight. I listen carefully to his words.

Cross my path on your way downtown.
Beware the lady all dressed in brown
'Round the corner and down the road.
Tell me your burdens and I'll carry your load.

I think of the most dangerous places in Port-au-Prince— Cité Soleil, La Saline, and even some dark corners in Delmas and La Ville. They don't compare to this empty, sparsely lit road called American Street where only a dog barks and an old man sings before the break of dawn. I tiptoe down to the front closet and pull out the first coat and boots I find. The coat must be one of Pri's, since it hangs wide and loose over my body. Slowly, I open the door and walk down the front steps and to the corner.

Bad Leg only hums now and I'm a few steps away. I don't get too close. "Mister?" I ask.

He keeps humming.

"Excuse me, mister?"

He stops humming and stares down Joy Road.

"Sir, I'm here. I just came to ask you about your leg."

"Welcome to American Joy, little lady." He sings these words, too, in his deep American southern accent.

"What happened to your leg?" I ask again.

"I left it on the other side." He laughs a dry, grainy laugh—not like his singing voice. "Forgot to take it with me. Went to visit my daddy, who first moved here back in sixty-one. He was looking for that American joy that everybody said was up here in Motor City—Motown. Thought it meant mo' money! You, too? Daddy had the sugar. His left leg was eaten up so bad, it looked like pork sausage."

"Bad. Leg," I whisper to myself, trying to make sense of what he is saying.

"So when I went over to the other side to see him, he asked to borrow my good left leg. That was when I was a fine young thing—had all my teeth. You don't go over to the other side with your whole body. You gots to keep it right here—like a wet coat or muddy shoes before you walk up into somebody's nice house. So you're nothing but hot air and memory over there on the other side. I was walking around just fine with my missing leg. Thought I'd given my daddy the memory of a leg—you know, give him back that feeling of walking on two feet instead of one good foot and a pork sausage. Till I got back home and was flesh and blood again. Tried to walk over to the kitchen to fry an egg and fell right on my face and lost my front teeth at the same time. My left leg was still intact, all right, but its soul was all gone. Couldn't move it, bend it, kick. Shit! Could chop my leg off and wouldn't feel a thing 'cause it has no soul. I left it on the other side. It was as dead as Marvin Gaye."

"Leg. Bad," I say loud and clear, because I now see him for who he is—the old man at the crossroads with his hat and cane and riddles come to open doors for me. He is the *lwa* who guards the gates to everything good—to everything bad, too. "Bad. Leg. Legba. Papa Legba."

"Yep?"

"Please, Papa Legba. Why won't you let my mother through to this side?"

He doesn't answer. Instead, he closes his eyes and leans his body all the way to one side without falling off the bucket. His bad leg stretches out in front of him as dead as a fallen tree.

I rush back into the house because the cold threatens to swallow me whole. Back in Chantal's room, I light a tea candle and begin my prayers for my mother. I don't ring a bell or rattle the *asson*. Instead, Papa Legba, the keeper of the crossroads, the one who will open the gates for my mother, sings his song. It creeps through the windows.

> Pull up a chair, let's have a meal,
> Shuffle them cards, let's make a deal.

I'll give you the key and set you free,

Be right here waiting for just a small fee.

Beware the lady all dressed in brown.

Don't even know her way downtown.

"I know you're not really listening to that crazy man." Chantal rolls over, awake.

I miss the last words of Papa Legba's song. I rush to the window to see if he's still there, but Papa Legba is gone. All that's left is the plastic bucket.

"He's Papa Legba," I say. "He sits at the crossroads and he holds a cane."

"That's what Ma used to say when we were little. That man has been there at that corner just about all my life. But he comes and goes."

"So why don't you ask him for help?"

"'Cause he's a crazy old man, that's why. He's not a *lwa* and he's not magical. Now can you please go to sleep?"

I don't. I stay up until the morning sun reaches me. I will set my mother free. Papa Legba, the one who stands at the center of all crossroads and in front of all doors, will make it so.

NINE

THE FOLLOWING FRIDAY, I pack a small bag for Manman—some underwear, toiletries, and her magic.

"You're planning to leave us already?" Chantal asks as she gets dressed.

"We have to get my mother," I say. "It's been too long. I have to find out what's going on. Your mother is not doing anything."

"She is. Trust me. She didn't go through all that trouble bringing her over here just to leave her hanging. We want Aunt Val here, too, you know."

"How can I go to New Jersey?" I ask.

Chantal sighs. "You'd have to take the Greyhound for, like, fifteen hours. But you're not going anywhere. And I'm not taking you to New Jersey. Ma is finding everything out. If she say to wait, then you wait. If she say to move, then you move. But I see that you're hardheaded like your cousins."

"And you are not?"

She turns to me and looks me straight in the eyes. "When I was sixteen, I left home and told my mother I was going to find my father's killer. I was gone for six days."

I don't say anything for a long minute, waiting for her to finish the story. "Well, did you find him?"

"Yeah," she says. "So we're family, all right. But I'm not gonna let you do anything stupid. Okay?"

After school, Pri doesn't leave me alone. She follows me from my last class to my locker and out the door. Maybe she thinks that I will do like Chantal and disappear for six days. I've been thinking about it since this morning. I can do it. I have enough money. It will only take two busses and lots of hours to pick up my mother and come back.

"Do you even know where Jersey is?" she asks, as if she's reading my mind. "How are you gonna tell the difference between New Jersey and motherfuckin' Wisconsin?"

"I know English, I can read, and I have money," I say as I walk down the front steps of the school.

"Do you even know the shit that happens to dumb-ass girls like you who wanna go on road trips? They get snatched and thrown in the backs of vans and forced to turn tricks," Pri says, huffing and puffing as she tries to keep up with me.

I stop when I reach the sidewalk. "Turn tricks? You mean prostitution? They do that to girls in Haiti, too. And it hasn't happened to me."

"Your voodoo is not gonna save you out here on these streets."

"Pri," I say, looking straight into her eyes. "No one is helping me with my mother. She's in a prison. *Prison!* Her only crime was coming here to this country to make a better life for us. So I know she's counting on me. I have to help her."

Pri shoves her hands into her coat pockets, cocks her head back, and looks down her nose at me. "You gonna be all right, cuzz?"

I nod. "Yes, Pri."

She inhales, pulls the hood of her coat over her head, and looks around as if searching for someone. "Look. Chant ain't here yet and Donna left early with her man. He offered to take us home, but I wasn't trying to get into that nigga's car. Chill at the school for a minute, and meet me out here in, like, fifteen. And you're not going to no damn New Jersey!"

She goes over to a group of girls standing near the school. I don't recognize any of them and they don't have our uniforms on. Again, I'm left out of my cousins' circle and I know for sure that I'm not the Fourth Bee.

I return to the CVS for only a few minutes until it's time to meet up with Pri again. I make a mental checklist of all the things I want to buy this time: more toiletries for myself, hair stuff, and maybe a magazine.

I'm in one of the wide aisles when a woman's voice makes me jump and drop a jar of hair moisturizer on the floor.

"Hey!" she calls out. "I keep running into you."

It's the woman from last week with the same fuzzy hat, but this time she's wearing a brown coat. She comes over to me and I wonder if she lives in the neighborhood.

I don't say anything and glance at the few other people in the aisle.

"You know, I'm looking for a good high school for my niece," the woman says. "How do you like that school?"

"It's okay," I say, and move on to the next row of products on the shelf.

"Those are some real good kids over there. Not too much trouble."

I look down at her boots—the same clean leather boots as before. Manman told me not to judge people by their clothes but by their shoes. A wise person will only be left with threads, but their shoes should be made for endless walking in search of a better life. "If you already know that the school is good, then why are you asking me?"

She laughs. "Smart cookie. It's always good to get an inside perspective, you know?"

I pick up the colorful jar, place it back on the shelf, and walk away.

"Wait. You are Donna's cousin, right?"

I stop. I don't turn. I wait for her to explain herself.

"I need to talk to you."

"How do you know Donna?" I ask, only turning a little just to see her face.

She shrugs. "I also know Pri and Chantal, and their mother, Marjorie. I'm familiar with their case from several years back. Their father, your uncle, was killed near the Chrysler plant."

I stand frozen for a moment because this is the first time I've heard someone actually say these words—*your uncle was killed*.

I turn to face her full-on. I look into her eyes and decide to trust her because she knows this important part of our story.

The restaurant the lady takes me to is within walking distance from the school, so I can always run back if anything happens. Besides, I didn't even know there was somewhere nice to eat so close to the school. It's a Mexican restaurant that serves rice and beans and I'm happy to finally get to eat something familiar.

She sits across from me at a booth. I keep on my coat, but she removes hers. She wears a white shirt, a blue sweater, light makeup on her brown skin, a simple wedding ring, and an endless smile. "Please, order as much as you want. I invited you here for a chat, so it's good manners that I treat you to a meal." Her voice is even and firm.

"Have you come here with my cousins?" I ask.

She exhales. "Actually, I have not." She wipes her hands on a napkin and extends one out to me. "I'm Detective Shawna Stevens with the Grosse Pointe Park Police Department."

I freeze and press my back against the seat. I start to slide out and contemplate leaving the restaurant.

"Wait a minute. You haven't done anything wrong. This isn't about you or your cousins. I just need your help," she says. "And I can help you with your mother."

I settle back into my seat. My skin, muscles, and bones feel as if they have melted away and I can simply step out of my body. "My mother? You can help?"

"Yes," she says, nodding.

I smile at her. But my smile quickly fades as I realize that Papa Legba may open doors, but sometimes he leads you through a labyrinth. "How do you know about my mother and what do you want from me?"

She goes into her bag and pulls out a newspaper. Right there on the front page is a picture of a blond girl. I've seen her before, on the TV and on other newspapers lying around at school. The headline reads: PROTESTS SCHEDULED OUTSIDE DETROIT POLICE DEPARTMENT FOR THE DEATH OF GROSSE POINTE PARK TEEN.

I shrug. "She was on drugs."

"Her name was Madison Helwig and she was seventeen years old. She died from a bad combination of designer drugs.

We're trying to find out how Madison and her friends got access to those drugs. And there's a whole community that wants someone to go down for her death. Do you know anything about drugs and drug dealers, Fabiola?"

I shrink back in my seat again. I start to answer her but she cuts me off.

"Of course you don't. Sure, you might've known some people in Haiti, but I think you know more of them now that you're in Detroit," she says. The waitress comes over to take our order, but Detective Stevens shoos her away.

My stomach twists into a knot. "I don't know anybody," I say.

She folds her hands in front of her and leans back in her seat. "Drayton Willis Carter. He goes by Dray."

My stomach sinks.

"He's Donna's boyfriend, right?"

I shrug.

"Look, we need to get this guy off the streets. He's selling drugs to these nice kids like you in and around Detroit. He's not a good guy, Fabiola. But we need proof. We need evidence that he's the one getting drugs into these parties. We need to catch him in the act."

I look all around the restaurant. "But that is your job," I say.

She inhales and looks around, too. "Yes, it is. But our work is not without the help of good American citizens like yourself. You are an American citizen, right?"

I nod slowly.

"And your mother is not," she goes on. "That's why they're keeping her at that detention center."

"But the American embassy gave her a visa. She didn't do anything wrong," I insist.

"You were born here after your mother's visa expired seventeen years ago. She wanted to make sure you were born American, that you could come back. Unfortunately, overstaying your visa is breaking the law. They think she might do it again."

I swallow hard and glance toward the exit. I recognize some kids from my school coming in, but they don't see me just yet.

"Fabiola, we can get her out. *And* we can expedite the process for her to obtain a green card. She won't have to hide once she's here. She can live and work legally. Isn't that what she wants? What you both want?"

I sit up in my seat, and it's as if my insides are like flowers that have blossomed after a tiny bit of rain. Something comes alive within me. But I wasn't born last night, as my mother would say. I remember how Manman would outwit those *vagabon* in suits who would offer expedited visas in exchange for things that are not meant to be given away for visas. "What will this cost?" I ask.

"No. No money. Just information . . . on Drayton. Dray. Your cousin's boyfriend."

I take a sip of water. "I think he hits my cousin. They call them D&D—Dungeons and Dragons. That's all I know."

"You've been inside that white BMW of his, right? Did you ever wonder what he does to have that kind of car? And does he buy your cousin nice things?"

Everything I've noticed about Donna flashes through my mind—her long coat, high-heeled boots, gold-rimmed sunglasses, fake hair, makeup, even her fancy underwear. I nod. Slowly.

"Sweetheart? Bottom line: no one around here is gonna talk. So this all becomes like some sort of chaotic cycle. Bad people stay on the streets, good people die; bad people make a shitload of money, good people have to scrape pennies."

"Same thing in Haiti," I say, really quiet.

"I'm sure. But here, you can actually make a difference. Look, you have your cousins, but you don't have to be loyal to *their* friends. You don't owe anybody anything, except your promise to your mother, right?"

I just look at her.

"We know that Dray goes out to these parties in the nice parts of town. We just need to know the next time he's going and to which party. Maybe you can ask Donna, or your other cousins. Not too hard, right? Just a time and a place." She slips her hand inside her coat, pulls out a business card, and slides it over to me.

The waitress comes back with her pad in hand. "You ready to order now?" she asks in a thick Spanish accent.

"I'll take my coffee to go. She'll have whatever her heart

desires," the detective says, and slaps a twenty-dollar bill on the table.

I slide the money back to her as she steps out of the booth. "You forgot something," I say, but I take the card and slip it into my wallet.

I retrace my steps back to the school, where the block is almost empty and most of the stores' gates are already down. A car honks behind me, making me jump, and I curse out the driver in my head. I turn around to see Broke Kasim roll down his window, flashing his bright, dimpled smile. I sigh, roll my eyes. The curse words in my mind have all disappeared, and maybe there are squiggly lines that want to form his name in pretty script letters with curlicues and flowers and stars and hearts and more hearts.

"Fabulous, I've been looking for you," he says. His voice is like a warm sea breeze filling up the cold, dry air in this place. "Where were you going? And why are you still at school?"

He shuts off the engine and gets out of the car from the driver's side and comes around to open the passenger-side door for me. But I don't go in.

"Pri was looking all over the place for you. I don't even know why they haven't given you a phone by now," he says.

Still, I don't go in.

"Come on, Fabulous. Get in. Pri went all the way down-town thinking you got on some bus to go to New Jersey."

With that, I slide into the passenger seat of his old and dirty car.

"Why would you want to go to New Jersey, anyway? Why not New York, or better yet, Chicago? Hell, it's closer."

"You ask too many questions," I say as I cover my legs with the bottom of my coat and place my book bag on my lap.

"Sorry about my car," he says as he moves junk from in between the seats. "We can't all be ballers like Dray and your aunt Jo."

"Ballers?"

"Money makers. High rollers. Ain't the president of Haiti a baller or rapper or something like that?"

My thoughts return to the woman with the brown coat, the detective. She said Dray was, like, a high roller, and that was bad.

He takes out his phone and dials a number. "Ay yo, I found her. . . . She was just standing in front of the school. . . . Yeah. . . . Hold on." He extends the phone out to me. "Pri wants to talk to you. She's pissed."

I don't really want to take it, so I slowly bring it up to my ear. I don't say anything, but she immediately starts to yell as if she already hears my breath.

"Where the fuck were you? Are you shittin' me right now? How you gonna straight disappear like that and don't tell nobody where you went? Matter of fact, somebody said they saw you go into the CVS and then leave with some lady. What the

94

fuck is that, Fabiola? You actin' like you runnin' these streets already. I done told you these bitches out here don't play. Even those Mexican bitches around the school will cut you if you . . ."

I give the phone back to Kasim. He doesn't know what to do with Pri's loud, dirty mouth.

"Ay yo, Pri? Pri? Calm down. You know who you sound like now, right? That's exactly how your mom used to go in on Donna back in the day. . . . Yeah, a'ight. You got a ride? Cool. . . . I'll take her home, then. . . . Don't worry. She's with me. She's in good hands." Kasim laughs. "I'm just messing with you."

It's quiet in the car for a long second after he hangs up with Pri. Then he says, "Yo, you really gotta tell somebody where you're going around here."

I don't look at him. I look ahead of me, then through the window next to me, but not at him. My thoughts are still simmering on that detective, Donna's boyfriend, Dray, and my mother.

"You hungry? Wanna grab some dinner with me?" He starts the car but lets it idle.

I turn away and look out the window, trying hard not to smile.

"I mean, no disrespect, Fabulous. I could just take you home," he says.

"No, it's okay," I say. "I can eat."

"I'm sure you can eat. Ever had Middle Eastern food before? Like kebabs, tabbouleh, falafels, and shit."

I smile. "I have Syrian friends back in Haiti. I miss them. My favorite food they make is baklava."

"*My favorite is baklava,*" he mocks me with a fake accent and laughs. "Don't tell me you're one of them bougie chicks. No wonder you call me broke. You need a man who's gonna buy you boxes of baklava and get you nice and thick. Put some meat on those little Haitian bones."

I laugh and hit him on his arm. He turns on the radio, but no sound comes through the speakers. He bangs on the dashboard and the music blares throughout the car. He turns the volume down and apologizes.

"See? I told you," I say. "Broke."

"I was waiting for you to say that." He laughs as he pulls away from the curb and makes a U-turn down Vernor Highway. "You can't tell by my car that I got stacks in the bank. I'm not gonna be one of those dudes rollin' up in no BMW and still live in their mama's basement. I'm trying to buy a condo next year, or one of them houses they're selling for, like, five bucks and fix it up real nice."

"Oh, yeah? So what do you do for work with all those *stacks* in the bank?"

"Been working since I was nine. Saved every penny. I can show you my job, if you want. The café across the street from the opera house. You been there? Maybe someday we'll go—do some bougie shit with my bougie girl."

"No, no, no, no. I am not your girl."

He laughs. "Who said I was talking about you? Did you hear me say Fabulous? No. See? You need to work on your English comprehension."

"But you said . . . Never mind," I say. I can't wipe the smile from my face, even as the time stretches thin and wide without another word being exchanged between us. I stare out the car window still smiling, and somehow, Detroit becomes more colorful than it's ever been. But something is tugging at me. I think of all that is still wrong—my manman in New Jersey. Detective Stevens and what she asked me to do.

His cell phone rings.

"Ay yo, what up, Dray?"

I try not to listen and let my mind wander to some other place where that emptiness lives. But his constant *yeah*s and *nah*s pull me into his conversation with this person who should be off the streets if what the detective lady said is true.

"Fab, we gonna have to cut tonight short, a'ight?" Kasim says, hanging up, turning toward me.

"It's okay," I say, shaking my head. "Just bring me home."

"Wait, wait." He takes one look at my face and pulls out his cell phone again. "Yo, Dray. I'll holla at you later, man. I can't roll through tonight."

Kasim hangs up and turns to me. "Let's go get something to eat. A'ight with you?"

My smile is even bigger now—a teeth-showing smile, as Manman would call it. But how could I even have a glimmer of happiness right now with my mother in jail for no reason? If only I could smile like Aunt Jo with half my face in a frown.

Kasim parks along a sidewalk that's lined with tall and wide buildings. When he turns off the engine, I start to open my door. But he stops me and says, "Wait, I got you."

He runs all the way to the other side of the car to open the door for me. The sign on the building in front of us reads BUCHAREST GRILL. I've been to a restaurant only once back in Haiti, and that was after my First Holy Communion. If my mother didn't cook, we'd go to a neighbor's house to get a plate of food in exchange for good neighborhood gossip. Already today, I will have gone to two restaurants. It is another reminder that my life here in Detroit could not be more different from home.

Kasim reaches for me as I step out of the car. His hand in mine is warm, and for a moment, I feel brand-new, as if like my cousin Primadonna, I am beginning to live up to this new name—Fabulous.

TEN

I DON'T LIKE the pita bread, and the bean dip is too cold. Hummus, they call it. Kasim devours a chicken breast topped with cabbage and pickles and other things I can't identify. Even in this Middle Eastern restaurant, I try to find some seed of home in every dish. There isn't enough spicy sauce on my sausage. The breads, salads, and pastas are all too dry. I only finish a small plate of curly French fries.

"What's up?" Kasim asks, chewing with his mouth open. "Food ain't fancy enough for you? Sorry ain't no baklavas that your *serious* friends back in Haiti make."

I giggle and a piece of food shoots out of my mouth and lands on the table. "Serious? You mean Syrian? From Syria." I laugh.

He keeps chewing and looking at me. Then he asks, "Do people move back to Haiti when they're old? Like retire with a house on the beach and shit?" He's serious now.

I nod. Then I shake my head. "I don't know. Maybe some people. But I don't have the right family name with a big business to inherit. My mother wanted to retire here."

"Retire here? In Detroit?"

"Uh-huh." I take a sip of my soda, but even that's not the same. Coca-Cola or Pepsi is only refreshing at the end of a long hot day. It makes no sense here with all this cold.

"That's crazy. People go to Florida or Georgia to finish out their last days. My pops, he's not old or anything, but he went back to Memphis. That's in Tennessee. You ever heard of Memphis? I was supposed to go back and live with him there, but . . . Detroit is home. Know what I mean?"

I nod. I don't really hear his words. His lips are nice and oily from his food and he licks them often. He has good table manners. He uses a knife and fork the way my teachers taught us at school. His fingernails are short and clean, and in between his fingers are not cracked and ashy. I've learned to notice these things about boys in Haiti. It tells me whether or not they live a hard life—if they use their hands to clean car windows for pocket change on the streets or to turn the pages of books in expensive schools. But here, I can't tell. He says he works at a café. He doesn't have the hands of someone who serves coffee all day. So I ask, "Do you read books?"

He laughs. "You're asking me if I'm literate? Didn't you just see me read the shit off the menu? You did hear me pronounce fucking chicken *shawarma* correctly, right?"

I sit back and wipe the smile off my face.

He just stares.

I stare back.

He laughs again. "I'm sorry, Fab. I just don't like when girls do that. Either they think I'm swimming in cash money, or they think I'm dumb as fuck. First you think I'm broke and then you're asking me if I can read?"

I open my mouth to say something, but my mind has not formed the words yet.

When the waitress passes, Kasim asks for the check. He's a little bit different now. I've offended him. I smile on the inside because I want to hold on to this bit of discomfort between us for a while. This is how I will get to know him, get to know what makes him angry or sad.

He quickly takes the check and pays for everything with cash. He doesn't look at me even as we leave the restaurant and get into the car. Before he starts it, I put my hand on his hand.

"I'm sorry, but that's not what I meant," I say. "I mean, do you like to read? Do you like school? Do you like studying?" I don't look at him, but I can tell from the corner of my eye that he doesn't like my question, or he doesn't know how to answer. He twists his mouth every which way to try to come up with an explanation for questions that only require a yes or a no.

Finally, he says, "I ain't never had a girl ask me that before. I mean, that's not some shit you ask a nigga from around here."

I wait for him to explain further. Then I ask, "Why not?"

"You think when Donna met Dray she asked him if he likes *studying*?"

"Dray did not take me out to dinner. You did. And I am not Donna."

"You don't get it. You're just too different. You're not from here."

"No, no, no. I understand. There are guys like Dray in Haiti, too. We call them *vagabon*, drug dealers. Maybe some of them like to study, but they love money more."

He laughs again. This time, as if I told a really good joke. "Yo, you trying to diss my man Dray? What makes you think he's a drug dealer?"

I want to swallow back my words. My face gets hot, hot. I've spoken too much. "I did not say he's a drug dealer."

"So you think I'm a drug dealer?"

"Are you?"

He laughs. "So I'm broke, I can't read, *and* I'm a dope boy."

"I did not say any of those things, Kasim. You seem like a nice person."

"And what about my boy Dray? You don't like him, do you?" He starts the car, but he waits for it to warm up.

"He's mean to Donna. How can you be friends with someone who doesn't respect his girlfriend?" I ask.

"I told you they got their own thing going on. And besides, me and Dray are not just friends. He's like fam. I know you can understand that with those crazy cousins of yours."

"So if he's family, are you going to do what he does, hit your girlfriend, too?"

He laughs. "Oh, you're on a roll tonight, shorty. I'm taking tabs." He holds up his hand and counts off his fingers. "Let's see . . . We got broke, illiterate, drug dealer, and now, girlfriend beater?"

I laugh and look out my window, which is all fogged up. This moment feels very good, but I almost don't want it. Something is missing. Maybe I don't want to be completely happy if everything is not right. I don't know if I can trust this boy. I take my finger and draw a line. I want to write a word or draw a picture, but a line is the only thing I come up with. Then I just wipe it all away and I can see the moon behind a tall building in the distance.

"I'm nothing like Dray," Kasim says quietly. "I don't hit girls. And I would never, ever disrespect you. Shit, I feel bad for even cursing around you. But that's just who I am. I want you to see the real me."

I don't turn to face him. I listen. There's honesty in his words now.

"Yeah, I sold some weed here and there for some change. I needed to hook my mother up so she could pay some bills, a new muffler for this piece-of-shit car over here, and maybe one day I'd want to go back to school. But I ain't no kingpin, know what I'm saying? So it's just favors here and there. Shit you do for fam."

A cold chill travels up my spine. *Shit you do for fam.* The way he says it, it's like he would do anything for his family, like for love and respect. I say it out loud. "Shit you do for fam." I turn to him.

"Shit you do for fam," he repeats.

The drive back to American Street is long and quiet. The silence swells between us and it's warm and comforting. When he pulls up to the house, he turns to me and doesn't smile. The sun has set and I can only see his face from the light of the distant moon. His eyes look sleepy, but they move all about my whole face. I let his eyes caress me, until he reaches over to move my braid away from my cheek.

He leans in. I lean in. He kisses me. He parts his lips, but I keep mine closed, and I slowly pull away. He's frozen there with his mouth slightly open, until he breathes. "Damn."

ELEVEN

"**DON'T GIVE IT** up too quick, though," Pri says as I'm changing out of my clothes. She's sprawled out on my air mattress wearing a hooded sweatshirt and sweatpants—her at-home uniform. A pair of big blue headphones hangs around her neck.

"Oh, Princess!" I say, as if she's just accused me of being a *bouzin*, a whore.

"It's Pri, *Fabulous*! So. You gonna let Kasim smash that or make him wait?"

"*Smash*? He will not *smash* anything!" I say.

"Good. He's nice and all, but make him sweat and beg."

"Leave her alone!" Donna calls out from the bathroom. "Don't listen to her. Why don't you worry about your own love life, Pri."

"No, Fab, don't listen to *her*. Donna will buy you lingerie and shit and even book you two a hotel room if you leave it up to her," Pri says.

"No, I won't!" Donna yells.

Pri shakes her head and gestures for me not to believe anything Donna says.

I giggle and ask, "Do you have a love life, Pri?"

"Yes, she does!" Donna calls out again. "She can't even step to the girl she likes."

Pri quickly gets up from the mattress. "Thanks a lot, D!"

"Wait," I say. "You like somebody?"

"Don't ask me no dumb-ass questions, Fabulous."

I stand in front of her. I don't want her to leave. I want her to talk to me the same way she did when I was braiding her hair. "Do you need new braids?" I ask.

"So you can be all up in my business?"

"What's her name?"

"None of your *business*."

"Her name is Taj," Donna says. The bathroom door is closed, but she can still hear everything we're saying.

"Would you please cut that shit out, D!" Pri shouts. "Damn. And wipe that smile off your face, Fabulous. It ain't like that."

Chantal's heavy footsteps rush up the stairs, home from her college classes. It's as if a cloud of cold air has followed her into the house, and I shiver in my pajamas. "What y'all getting on about?"

"Kasim took Fab out to dinner," Pri says. She settles back down on my air mattress and I sit on Chantal's bed. "Like a restaurant, for real for real."

"If he asks you to marry him, say no," Chantal says as she drops her heavy book bag on the floor and takes off her coat.

"Marriage? We're talking about fucking and you roll up in here talking about *marriage*? Fuck outta here with that shit!" Pri throws a pillow at her big sister.

I giggle and throw a pillow at Pri just for fun. She throws it back. I try to duck, but it hits me in the face.

"Did you tell her how Kasim always falls in love and wants to buy wedding rings for his girlfriends?" Chantal asks. She starts taking out books and her computer from her bag before she even undresses.

"What?" I say. "Wedding rings? He's only . . . Wait. He's seventeen, right?"

"Eighteen, so he's old enough to get married if he wants," Chantal says. "Wait, I got something for you." She hands me a box from her book bag.

"Married? No way," I say as I open the unmarked box. I can't hide the smile on my face, because the thought of getting married makes my insides like syrup. It all plays out in my head like a very fast commercial—picking out a dress with my mother, getting my hair done in a salon, seeing my cousins fight over which bridesmaid dress they want to wear, going on a honeymoon to Italy or Miami.

The box holds a brand-new cell phone, and I immediately turn it on and start pushing all the buttons.

"Look at her face! Now you can text Kasim your wedding plans, 'cause you were seriously thinking about it, weren't you?" Pri says.

I quickly snap out of it as Donna comes into the room and all my cousins start to laugh at my expression.

Then Donna asks, "Are you a virgin, Fab?"

I smile and nod. "A little something here and there, but . . . my mother would kill me."

"No dick? Good, stay that way," Chantal says.

Pri kisses her teeth. "Fab, *mother* and *dick* are two words that should not be in the same conversation. And ain't nobody wanna be like your corny ass, Chant. If you could fuck a book, you would."

"You know what?" Chantal comes over and shoves Pri's head. "I would fuck a book before I fuck some dude who doesn't respect me. I'd fuck a degree, a paycheck, and a damn career! And Fab, you better act like your mother *is* here. Don't do anything she wouldn't want you to do."

"Yeah, listen to your mother, Fab, and not corny-ass Chantal," Pri says.

My cousins go back and forth with their jokes and playful insults. Pri takes another pillow and starts hitting her sisters. They each do the same. I grab a pillow to cover my face so I can laugh and laugh. My whole body feels strange. My heart doesn't beat; it dances. It's as if Kasim has stepped into my mind and invaded every single thought.

As everything calms down, Pri lies on Chantal's bed, breathing heavily and still giggling. Donna is at the dresser mirror, messing with her hair. And Chantal is at the edge of her bed with an opened book and a highlighter in her hand. While their attention is away from me, I let my thoughts wander—Kasim, Kasim, Kasim.

"Aww, she likes him," Donna says, coming over to my mattress and plopping down next to me. "He's sweet. He'll take care of you."

"Get away from her, D," Chantal says, not looking up from her book.

Donna waves a hand at her. "It's all about love, Fab, I swear," she says. "If he loves you, he'll make you feel like a million dollars."

I suddenly wonder if Dray really loves Donna. I don't think it's love that makes her feel like a million dollars—but maybe the actual money he gives her for all those wigs and makeup and clothes. Drug money, if what the detective said is true. If Kasim could make me feel like a million dollars, then I want it to be a million dollars of love and not actually a million dollars.

"Do you love Dray?" I ask suddenly.

The room gets quiet.

"Of course I do," Donna says.

There are no more jokes and laughs after that.

I must be the only one who can hear Bad Leg's song tonight. Chantal is as still as a rock on her bed, and the window is closed. His song is loud, but I can't understand his words. I toss every which way trying to shut out his voice. My eyes are weary, my thoughts are on overtime, refusing to let me sleep. Everything and everyone swims around my mind like ghosts in a haunted house—the detective lady and her proposition, Kasim and his "shit you do for fam," and the love that Donna has for a bad guy who sold drugs that killed a girl. I am being forced to make a choice.

I know that my prayers will ease my heart, so I get up. My legs take me down the steps, to the coat closet, out of the house, and to the corner of American and Joy.

"What should I do?" is the first thing I ask Papa Legba. I need straight answers, so I ask a straight question.

He's quiet. There are sirens in the distance. A dog barks. The wind howls around me and I realize how strange this place is with all these little houses, and on most days, I barely see any people. If there was a place like this back in Haiti, everyone would come out and gather on the sidewalk to exchange meals and gossip. No one would be left alone in a tiny house with only their regrets and sorrows to keep them company.

Papa Legba finally begins.

Crossroads, cross paths,
Double-cross and cross-examine,
Cross a bridge across my mind.
A cross to bear across the line,
And cross the street across town.
Cross out, cross off,
cross your t's and cross your fingers,
then nail him to a cross
as you cross your heart
and hope not to die.

A cigar appears in his hand. He's never had it before. He takes a pull and exhales thick white smoke that swirls up into the air like a cloud. I watch it bend and stretch like a slow-turning cyclone until it stops at the street signs—where Joy Road meets American Street.

Joy and American. A crossroads. Intersecting. One is not the other. I look down Joy Road with its few streetlights dotting the wide path. There are not that many houses and lots of open land. It can either mean endless possibilities or dark, empty hope.

I look down American Street with its houses in neat rows and the open lots like missing teeth. I know so many people back in Haiti, so many families who would kiss the ground and thank Jesus for a street like this, especially one named American.

My two paths meet at this corner, and it seems like I have to choose one. One street represents a future, the other leads to a different kind of life. Papa Legba, the keeper of the crossroads, will help me choose.

"On American Street, I will live with my aunt Jo and my cousins, and go to school, and have a cute boyfriend, and keep my mouth shut because in Haiti I learned not to shake hands with the devil. But on Joy Road, I will tell the truth. The truth will lead to my happiness, and I will drive long and far without anything in my way, like the path to New Jersey, to my mother, to her freedom, to my joy. Which road should I take, Papa Legba?"

When I turn back to the streetlight, he is gone. The light only shines on the overturned plastic bucket and the dancing smoke. It's beginning to feel as if I'm speaking to stagnant air—the spirits are just standing there without delivering my message to God.

"Where were you?" Chantal whispers as I quietly slide back onto my air mattress.

"Eating something in the kitchen," I lie.

"Yeah, right. You trying to get killed out here on these streets?"

"Killed?" I say. "I feel safer here than I did in Port-au-Prince."

Chantal laughs. I wait for her to stop, but she keeps going.

Then she sits up on her bed to face me. I can see the outline of her head in the moonlight.

"You ever seen a kid get stomped in the face. With boots?"

"No," I say. "Not stomped in the face. But beaten with a baton on the back by the police."

"Oh, y'all got police brutality, too?"

"It was because of the *manifestation* before the election. What you would call a protest, like the one for that girl who died because of drugs. Did they find out who gave her those drugs?"

She's quiet. Then she says, "Does it matter? She took them, right? If somebody hands you drugs and you take them, who's to blame? What, there are no drugs in Haiti?"

"Of course there are. And drug dealers, too. But they don't always have to deal drugs. There are other things to sell."

"Well, did you ever have to dodge bullets?"

"During *kanaval*. Some people were jumping on cars to dance and have a good time. But MINUSTAH thought they were making trouble. So they shot and we ran."

"Okay," she says, settling back down on her pillow. "Do you know what a dead body smells like? I mean, after it's been dead for, like, days."

"Yes. I remember the earthquake very well," I say, quiet, almost whispering.

"All right, then. You win."

"No, I don't. I lose. I am not home now. I left it behind. You are home."

"Home? No, I'm not. I wasn't born here. Haiti is home."

I shake my head, but she doesn't see me. "You would rather be in Haiti?"

She sighs and turns over on her bed to face me again. "Sometimes I wonder what my life would've been like if my father had never sent for me and my mother when I was a baby. Like, maybe the twins would never have been born. And your mother would not have come here to give birth to you. And maybe we'd be like sisters. We'd go to the beach every day, and eat good Haitian food, and go shopping for jeans and American clothes, and whatever we needed to know about America, we'd see it in the movies."

Now it was my turn to laugh. "The nice beaches cost money, and the public beaches are dirty and crowded. There are no movie theaters, and to go to a shopping center with nice clothes, we would have to take a bus for eight hours to the Dominican Republic."

"That's not true," she says. "I saw your pictures on Facebook. You were doing good. Especially with Ma's money."

"Well, me and my friends, we did different things. Not movies and malls. Not much in the city, in fact. I rode my bike through the streets of Les Cayes, rode donkeys up the mountainsides near Cap-Haïtien, and the beaches we went to were not resorts. We shared the ocean with fishermen and washerwomen. And we gossiped and joked. And fought. I had to fight a lot, because people knew we were getting money from family abroad. Manman was tired of fighting. She wanted her own money. She wanted to see her sister. She wanted me to be like you."

"Like me?"

"Matant Jo talked about you when she called. She said you were going to be the very first doctor in the family. Is it true? You're going to be a doctor?"

She pauses, then sighs. "Don't worry about me. Just make sure you get through your junior year. And stop messing with Bad Leg. And don't go around asking about that white girl. Please."

I nod, but she can't see me in the dark. I rest my tired head on her last words, letting them be my pillow.

CHANTAL'S STORY

What if memory is like a muscle? My anatomy & physiology class tells me how the human body works, but it can't tell me how the human mind works—not the brain, but the thoughts and memories.

I remember being nine years old, translating newspaper articles for my mother about my father's murder. I remember everything about that day those detectives walked into our house and I had to sit there and listen to every detail and tell it back to my mother in Creole. I had to do it the other way around for those insurance people from Chrysler—translate my mother's demands from Creole into English.

Creole and Haiti stick to my insides like glue—it's like my bones and muscles. But America is my skin, my eyes, and my breath. According to my papers, I'm not even supposed to be here. I'm not a citizen. I'm a "resident alien." The borders don't care if we're all human and my heart pumps blood the same as everyone else's.

I try to walk a path that's perfectly in between. On one side are the books and everything I have to do to make myself legit, and on the other side are the streets and everything I have to do to stay alive out here.

Ma wanted me to go to a big university. She told me not to worry about her and my sisters, to just do my own thing. But how could I? This is home. My mother is home. My sisters are home. And even you . . . you force me to remember the home I left behind. You make me remember my bones.

TWELVE

"FABIOLA, YOUR WRITING is good, but I have to give you a low grade because you didn't back up any of your claims," my English teacher, Mr. Nolan, says, looking at my paper and not at me.

I wonder if he can see a reflection of my face on that paper—if he can see me, my whole story. "Claims?" I ask.

"You were supposed to write a research paper, not a personal essay," he says, handing me back the homework. "There are some interesting ideas here, but they're unsubstantiated. You need to gather some sources, use quotes, and add a 'Works Cited' page. Use textual evidence."

He quickly gathers up his things on his desk and leaves the classroom. English is the last class for the day, so I thought there'd be time for him to explain everything to me. I've been writing essays and poems in English my entire life. I went to an English school in Haiti. It doesn't make sense that my paper isn't perfect.

I stare at all his markings, comments on the sides, question marks, whole sentences crossed out. I feel attacked because I wrote down everything I knew about the Haitian revolutionary hero Toussaint L'Ouverture and why he is important to me. But Mr. Nolan thinks everything I said was all wrong.

Someone coughs while I'm putting the essay back into my folder. Imani is standing in the doorway of the classroom. She already has on her coat and a gray scarf wrapped around half her face. "Why do you look like you're about to cry?"

"I'm not going to cry." I blink several times and swallow hard to make sure.

"Were you trying to get Mr. Nolan to help you? Waste of time," she says.

"I got a D on my paper," I tell her.

"A D? Did you write it in English? I mean, good English?"

"Of course I did! I know how to write in English!" I rush past her and into the hallway. Other students are making their way out, too, and I try to spot Donna or Pri in the crowd.

"Look, I always get As on my papers. I can take a look at yours, if you want."

At first I don't want Imani's help—I want to write essays perfectly by myself. But then I realize that writing papers for

Mr. Nolan is just another American system I need to game, as Pri would say. I never see Pri doing any schoolwork, but somehow she doesn't fail her classes. And Donna doesn't even carry a book bag. She takes a purse to school and I wonder what sort of magic she does to fit any books into it. Maybe Imani knows the answers. She always has a giant, heavy book bag as if she's selling goods at the market.

I stop and Imani almost bumps into me. "Yes," I say. "Please. I don't understand what Mr. Nolan wants. He says I'm a good writer, but I'm still doing something wrong."

"All right, let's go somewhere and I'll take a look at it. You can pay me back by getting me something to eat."

I don't question why Imani always wants to make sure I'm okay, and offers to help me with my schoolwork. I'm only thankful; this is one door Papa Legba has opened for me—friendship. Imani has big opinions about the world, and maybe she clings to me because I listen. I am amused by everything she says—McDonald's food is really plastic, downtown Detroit will be all white in ten years, the government watches us through our cell phones. I only laugh when she tries to prove it by showing me an article or video on the internet. Maybe she and Kasim can be friends, too, because he likes to talk about the same things.

I text Kasim for the address to the café. He always asks me to come see him, but I never wanted to have Chantal take me over. Now that I have a friend, I get to taste a slice of this Detroit freedom. But I still let Chantal know where I am and that Kasim will take me back home.

Imani and I walk to the corner of our school's block to catch the bus that goes down Vernor Highway. Once on the bus, I start to walk to the back, but Imani pulls my arm toward a seat next to her.

"Always sit close to the bus driver," she whispers.

I think of the small *tap-tap* trucks in Port-au-Prince where Manman told me to sit near the back so I can jump out in case anything happens.

"He's your boyfriend, Fabiola?" Imani asks after I tell her that we're going to see Kasim at his job.

I shake my head. But the smile on my face tells a different answer.

"Don't lie to me. I'm trying to help you out. Now, since you'll be meeting up with your boyfriend after school and all, this is the forty-nine bus and it goes down Vernor until you get to Twenty-First. Then you're on Bagley. We're gonna get off on Bagley and Walsh and walk to Michigan Avenue. Got it?"

I take note of this bus and the places it passes. The streets are even wider here, and there don't seem to be enough cars and enough people to fill up all the space. The sky stretches long and wide, and maybe this bus can go to the very edge of the world—or at least to my mother in New Jersey. I jump when

Imani calls my name, and I don't notice that fifteen minutes have gone by. Maybe she was talking all this time, but my mind was on the wide, endless roads.

When we're off the bus, we walk a few blocks to Kasim's café and stand outside. We watch through the wide window as Kasim serves coffee behind the counter.

"He is so cute. I've seen him around. He comes to the school with Donna's boyfriend."

I stop smiling. "Do you know Donna's boyfriend?"

"Dray? Who *doesn't* know Dray? He makes my skin itch. I don't know what your cousin sees in him. He looks good and all, but he still be looking at girls even when he comes to pick Donna up. And the guys at school can't even say hi to Donna when he's around. Dray was checkin' for her way back when we were in middle school. And he'd bring a different friend each time so they could hook up with her friends. All these girls would hang around Dray's car like he's a celebrity. Not me."

"Did Kasim . . . what did you say . . . hook up with a girl?"

"Nobody really liked Kasim 'cause he wasn't a baller. You could tell by his clothes and sneakers that Dray wasn't even trying to hook him up with dough, talkin' about everybody has to earn that shit. Looks like Kasim is doing just fine without Dray's dough."

"Dough?"

"Cash. Money. Dang, Fabiola! Do I have to translate *everything*? What are your cousins teaching you?"

We both laugh until the door to the café opens and Kasim's smile reaches me and warms my whole body.

"May I help you, ladies?" he says with a fake deep voice as he holds the door open while we walk in.

"We have to do some homework," I say, trying to hide my smile.

We sit down at an empty table, and I avoid talking to Kasim because he's supposed to be working. Imani removes her coat and unloads her bag, and I take out my essay but keep my coat on. I don't like how I look in my uniform. Imani starts to tell me how to fix my essay, but my eyes are glued to Kasim. He's extra friendly to the customers and smiles too much. He whistles while he pours coffee and other hot drinks from a machine. Every few seconds, he turns to me and smiles, or winks, and once, blows a kiss.

Imani kicks me under the table. I snap out of it and try to turn my attention to the essay. "Mr. Nolan said this is not a research paper. I have to put in *textual evidence*," I say as if I've been listening to her the whole time.

"I can't believe you brought me here just so you can make googly eyes at your boyfriend," Imani says. "You didn't hear a word I said. I just told you the same thing."

I can't fool her, so I laugh. She laughs. A white couple next to us shoots us looks, and we cover our mouths and laugh some more. Kasim comes over and places two mugs of hot chocolate on our table. He purposely touches my hand and tiny, sharp things travel all up and down my skin. Imani teases me, we sip on our warm drinks, Kasim keeps finding reasons to come to our table, we giggle some more, and the couple sitting next to us finally moves to another table.

I am like air now. Or a bubble. Delicate. I can pop at any time.

And I do.

When Imani gets up to use the bathroom, I pull out my wallet to pay for the hot chocolates. A card falls out onto the table. I turn it over to see the name Detective Shawna Stevens in bold, black letters. I tap the edge of the card on the table thinking if I should make the first move. She already knows where I go to school, and I'm sure she knows where I live. I glance out the wide window and wonder if she is watching me from some hidden place right now. This Detective Stevens called me a smart cookie, but she's a whole smart cake. Of course my cousins would not want to tell on Dray because they've known him for so long. But me, she knows that I don't care about that guy, especially if he cheats on my cousin and is mean to her. And most important, she knows that I want nothing more right now than to have my dear manman with me.

I try to be like air again. But thinking of my mother is like a long rope keeping me tied to earth.

THIRTEEN

I LEAVE A twenty-dollar bill on the table for Kasim, but he slides it back to me when he comes to pick up the mugs from our second set of hot chocolates. Imani and I are the only ones left in the café now. They let us stay long after they locked the front door to count the register and clean the machines.

"So you're gonna actually have to do some research," Imani continues. "Citing your sources means that you have to show proof of where you got your information. And make it look good. You can't just go on Wiki."

"Proof?" I ask. "Everything must have proof?"

"Yeah, and you have to—" Imani starts to say. But a loud thumping seems to make the whole building shake. Music. Heavy. It sounds as if giant speakers are suddenly on the sidewalk directly outside the café. Instead of covering her ears like me, Imani starts bopping her head and swinging her hand in the air. "That's my shit!" she says.

I watch as Kasim heads for the door, unlocks it, and walks outside to a slow-approaching white car. My stomach sinks. Dray. The tinted passenger-side window rolls down and Kasim leans in. Dray reaches over to give him something. I move in my seat to get a better look, but I still can't see. Kasim quickly comes back in and waves for us to come out.

"We gotta close up now. Wait for me outside, a'ight?" he says as I brush past him.

Dray turns down the music and comes out of his car wearing dark sunglasses, a black cap, and a gold-cross chain. He checks each of his tires, then pulls out a cloth from the trunk and wipes down the big, shiny silver things along the insides of the tires.

"Those really are twenty-twos," Imani whispers next to me, making me jump a little.

"Twenty-two what?" I whisper back, keeping my eyes on Dray.

"Twenty-two-inch rims. Hardly any room for the tires. When we were in middle school, he just had some hubcaps."

"Rims? Hubcaps? Do they cost a lot of money?"

"For a BMW? Hell yeah!" Imani's eyes are glued to Dray's car. And he must've noticed, because he's wiping every inch as if he's making it pretty just for Imani.

"You wanna take a picture?" he says, leaning back on his car and biting his bottom lip.

Imani shakes her head no.

"Come on. Do it for the 'Gram." Dray takes out his cell phone.

I can see that Imani doesn't want to. Dray gestures for her to come over even though she shakes her head again. Dray is trying to control her like he controls Donna. Imani drops her book bag and slowly walks over to him. I wonder if her skin is itching now. I want to stop her, but Dray grabs Imani's hand and gets down on one knee next to one of the rims, pulling her down with him. She almost stumbles but lands on his lap. He extends his phone and takes a few pictures of Imani on his lap, himself and his dark sunglasses, gold teeth, and gold chain, and expensive rims. Imani walks away really fast when Dray lets her go.

"You want one, too, Fabulous?" Dray asks just as Kasim walks out of the café and pulls down the gate.

I'm relieved when Kasim comes over and puts his arm around me. He pulls me in and kisses my forehead. The only person who has ever done that is my mother and, when I was little, my aunties in my old neighborhood.

"Aw, shit!" Dray says, leaning against his car. "Fabulous and my man Ka. That's what I'm talking about!"

"Dray said he's gonna give us a ride. You cool with that?" Kasim asks.

I turn to Imani. She shakes her head.

"Yo, what's your name, shorty?" Dray takes off his sunglasses, and he's still wearing his eye patch underneath. He licks his lips, and his good eye looks Imani up and down as if she's a piece of freshly fried *griot*.

"Imani," she says.

"Come on. I'll take you home. Imani."

Imani turns to me and pops her eyes out as if this is all my fault.

"No. We're okay. We'll take the bus," I say, taking Imani's hand.

"Fabulous, I'm not gonna let y'all just take the bus," Kasim says.

I glance over at Imani again, and her eyes tell me that she's surrendered. Dray wins, so we both walk over to where Kasim is holding open the back door. I slide in first. Then Dray nudges Kasim.

"Imani. You could ride with me in the front," Dray says.

I start to pull Imani in with me, but Kasim has already taken what was supposed to be her spot next to me. I want to say something, anything, but by the time the courage rises to my throat, Imani is in the passenger seat of Dray's car and the door is closed.

Heavy bass music blasts in my ears. From my spot behind Dray, I can see his whole face in the rearview mirror, and even though it's dark outside, he's put his sunglasses back on. Kasim tries to talk to me, but I can only keep my eyes on Imani, who has pressed herself against the car door trying to be as far away from Dray as possible. In the café, this song was "my shit." But now, she's as still and quiet as stone. Even as Dray inches his hand toward her lap.

Kasim tries to do the same and I turn my head away from him each time he comes closer to whisper something in my ear or kiss me. I want to say that it's not him. It's this car. It's his friend—his fam. It's Dray.

I'm so distracted that I don't even notice when we reach American Street. I thought we were going to drop off Imani first. But Dray finally turns down the music, and loud yelling takes the place of the heavy bass. My cousins. I can't tell which one. But all I hear is "Get the fuck out of the car, bitch!"

"Oh, shit!" Kasim whispers, and he quickly opens the door on his side.

I get a glimpse of Chantal and Pri coming out of the house. Then the passenger-side door swings open and it's Donna reaching in to pull Imani out. She grabs the sleeve of her coat, but Imani fights back.

"Oh, shit!" I say, for the first time in my life. I jump out of the car and aim straight for Donna. "No, no. Donna, leave her." I try to pull her hand away from Imani.

"Dammit, Fab! Get the fuck away from her!" Pri yells.

"Bitch, you're gonna take advantage of my cousin just so

you can fuck my man?" Donna yells. She manages to get Imani out of the car and finally lets her go.

Imani's eyes and mouth are wide. She fixes the sleeve of her coat and doesn't say a word to defend herself.

"No! That's not true!" I yell.

Donna ignores me and goes around to Dray and gets in his face. "You posting pictures on Instagram with bitches on your lap, Dray? And you had to do it with a bitch from my school on top of that?"

"Pri, Imani didn't want to," I say to my cousin.

Pri has come to stand beside me. "Go inside," she says, quietly, with fire in her eyes. Not for Imani, thank goodness. For Dray.

I won't leave my friend. I go to pull her away from the chaos of Dungeons and Dragons.

"Oh, hell no! You're not getting her outta this, Fab!" Donna yells. "She's guilty, too!"

"No!" I yell back. "She didn't want to take that picture and she didn't want to sit there. Leave her alone!"

"Yo, check your girl, Ka," Dray says to Kasim, who's been standing there like a useless tree stump.

Donna shoves Dray and puts a finger in his face. Chantal finally comes over to pull Imani away. I go to my friend, whose arms are frozen at her sides. "I'm sorry," I say to her.

"Imani, where you live?" Chantal asks her.

"Over there on Montgomery and Lawton," she says. "Please

tell Pri and Donna not to beat me up. I swear, I wasn't trying to get with Dray."

"Pri's not even thinking about you. And don't worry about Donna. You'll be all right."

With that, my stomach settles. I would have to fight my own cousins if they tried to hurt Imani. She's been more of a friend to me at school than they have.

Then Pri rushes past us toward the house while saying, "I ain't staying around to watch that shit. She's gonna get all up in his face, then next thing you know, she's coming home in the morning with a fucking black eye."

Just as she says this, Dray grabs Donna's neck and shoves her against the car with a loud thud. Both Chantal and I run to Donna just as Kasim rushes toward them and tries to get in between.

"Calm down, man. Calm down!" Kasim yells in Dray's face.

Chantal pulls Donna away, who is now holding her head down with her arms crossed. And Dray keeps yelling, even as Kasim extends his arms to keep him from getting too close to Donna again.

"You already know how I roll, D! It wasn't even like that!" he shouts with spittle coming out of his mouth.

My fists are clenched because rage burns through my whole body. I want to lunge at Dray's face, but Pri has beat me to it and is already yelling and cursing at him at the top of her lungs. Kasim holds her back until she pushes him off her, and then Dray begins to pace around his car.

My hot rage begins to melt. Maybe it's the cold. Maybe it's the way Dray holds his head and bends over as if he is about to let out a loud wail. Then I begin to see him for who he really is. Dray, with his sunglasses even as night spreads across the sky, and his gold cross gleaming, and his love/hate for my cousin, reminds me of the *lwa* Baron Samedi, guardian of the cemetery—keeper of death.

I hate him. I hate what he can do to my cousin. I hate that he is friends with the boy I'm beginning to like. I hate that he sells drugs that make people die. The detective's words ring in my ears—all she needed was information—the time and place of a party. If I can give her that, then maybe I can get this terrible man out of my cousin's life for good and get my mother back. An eye for an eye, and Dray has only one left.

Back in the house, I rush to the bathroom and pull out my cell phone, wallet, then the detective's card. Breathing heavily and with fire still raging inside of me, I stare at her name on the card for a long minute before I start texting. I send her my name and my new number. That is all for now.

I jump when someone bangs on the door. I stuff my phone and my wallet with the card in it back into my coat pocket and open the door. It's Donna with tears in her eyes.

PRIMADONNA'S STORY

You know why I go so hard for Dray? 'Cause he goes hard for me. I swear, ever since I was twelve years old, whatever I needed, Dray always came through. We were broken up for, like, six months back when I was a freshman, and he was seeing other girls and whatnot. But he still got me the things that I needed. It don't matter what those things were, he was just there. I mean, yeah, Pri looks out for me, too. But it's not the same. She be calling me a ho, and I know she's my twin and all, but it still hurts. How am I a ho when I've only been with one dude my whole life? Dray took my virginity, and he's still the same nigga I fuck with. For five years. How many hos can say that? You know, that's the shit I don't like about bitches. Just because everybody says I'm pretty and I wear nice clothes, it doesn't mean I'm a ho. But that reputation sticks to you like another layer of skin.

I remember when I was, like, ten, some of Ma's guy friends would come over and tell me that I'm gonna be "fast" just 'cause I was twitching in my little jeans. What the fuck? I was ten. And they'd say to my mother, Oh, she got a little body on her, so you gotta be packing to keep those boys away. But it wasn't my mother who was packing. It was Dray. He was the one who kept those boys away. Like that one time in the ninth grade, this dude from over on 6 Mile was going hard, coming to my school, and buying me flowers and shit. He was really cute, so I went on one date with him. But word got around that I slept with him. It got to Dray and he was pissed. I had to swear on my father's grave that the nigga didn't even get to kiss me. So Dray had to deal with him for spreading rumors about me. I found out the boy ended up in the hospital for a week. That's the shit Pri can't do. But Dray . . . After that, he bought me a diamond necklace and took me shopping. And it's been D&D all along. Dungeons and Dragons. Sometimes we fight each other, but he fights for me, and I fight for him.

FOURTEEN

"COME ON, FAB! Step up your hair game. You gotta actually look *fabulous* for people to start calling you Fabulous," Donna says, standing in front of me with one of her wigs.

I'm sitting on Chantal's bed as Donna tries to put that hairy thing on me and make my face look plastic again. I keep both my hands on top of my hair and shake my head like a toddler. "No!"

It's another Saturday night of us getting ready, but this time, I'm the only one going out. By myself. With Kasim. A date. A real date. I've been thinking about my mother all day. Would she approve? Would she like Kasim? Would she like what I was wearing? I don't even know if she would like me wearing wigs, or weaves, as Donna calls them, because I never so much as had braid extensions. Both me and Manman have managed just fine with our own hair—like Chantal and Pri.

My phone buzzes and I quickly grab it. It's Detective Stevens, and she texts that she'll be calling me at three o'clock tomorrow. Maybe I will tell her about Kasim. And maybe I will have some information for her. But I shake that thought from my mind, because tonight I don't want to have any worries.

"Who was that? Kasim?" Donna asks. "I think he'll like you more with a little more hair on your head."

I just nod.

"That's not true. You don't have to wear any of Donna's fake hair, Fab," Chantal says. She's spread out next to me on her bed, reading a textbook. "She's trying to make you look like her real twin."

"I heard that!" Pri says.

I stand up to look in the mirror. When I try to gather my thick braids up on top of my head, it's a mess.

"Come here," Chantal says, placing her laptop on her dresser. She punches a few keys, and soon we're on YouTube, watching a girl do her hair while giving instructions.

"Oh, lord." Donna sighs. "Chant has been on this natural-hair shit now and she's gonna try to make you look like Sasquatch." She plops down on the bed.

The girl in the video has thick hair like mine, and she pats it down with white cream from a jar that she displays on the screen. Then she parts and rolls and twists her hair into a fancy style. Chantal helps me do the same to my braids. When we're done, my hair looks so good that I could eat it. It's sculpted like a crown. I look like a goddess. Like Ezili herself, the *lwa* of beauty.

"Great." Donna sighs. "Now you look like Rosa Parks. Let's at least do your face so you look like Nicki Minaj."

"No!" I say, shaking my head. "No makeup."

"Dammit, Chantal!" Donna says. "There you go. You got your own twin now." She grabs her makeup box and wigs and leaves the room.

I don't know if she was joking or really angry that I liked the hairstyle.

"Ha-ha! You lost!" Pri yells to her. "Chantal and her corny-librarian hairdo won."

I only add lip gloss to my face. I lick my fingers and smooth down my eyebrows like my mother has done for me so many times. I look clean and decent. But now I have to find a good outfit to match my new hair. I search my mother's suitcase for one of her dresses—a red one with tiny flowers. It reaches to the middle of my calves, but otherwise, it fits perfectly.

"Oh, no," Pri says. "Don't tell me you're wearing that. Girls will jump you for going out with fine-ass Kasim and looking like a church lady."

"Leave her alone," Chantal says. "You look cute."

"Cute." Pri snorts under her breath. "As long as it helps you keep them legs closed and hold out for a long time. I mean, a long-ass time."

But I don't want to look like a church lady. I still want to look . . . good. So I take off my mother's church dress and put on a plain sweatshirt that belongs to Chantal and a pair of new jeans. I wear the Air Jordans that Pri picked out for me, but I keep my hairstyle. Now I don't look so . . . Haitian. So immigrant.

I fix my face in the mirror again to make me look serious, almost like Chantal's, a little bit like Pri's, with a touch of Donna.

"Okay. That's better, I guess," Chantal says. "Where's he taking you anyway?"

"I don't know."

"Well, if it's to his house, ask him to bring you back here right away."

"And if it's to someone else's house," Pri adds, "tell him 'Take me the fuck home!' Say it just like that. Let me hear you."

I know she's tricking me just so she can make fun of my accent and make me sound stupid. My curses are all wrong. My swag, as they call it, is off. But in my head, I sound just like them. I sound American.

I fix my lips and make a face until it feels just like Pri's, and I say, "Take me the fuck home!"

Both my cousins burst into laughter. Even Donna comes

into the room just to drop her body onto Chantal's, hold her belly, and laugh from a deep, joyful place. I look into the mirror and watch myself say those words over and over again, and each time, my cousins laugh harder.

"Yo, Fab! It's *fuck*. Not *fork*!" Pri manages to say between laughs.

When the doorbell rings, we all look out the window to see Dray's white car parked at the curb. Donna runs down to open the door and she calls my name. It's Kasim. He's driving Dray's car to take me on our date.

Kasim has flowers and he's dressed in a nice black coat, black pants, and shiny black shoes. His hair is shorter and neater and he's wearing glasses. He looks really good, but that car makes my insides feel like a hurricane. I don't want to get in, but I don't have a choice.

He must've seen me staring, because he says, "Dray told me I could use it. He likes you. He thinks we look good together." He rushes to open the passenger-side door. I look toward the corner where Bad Leg usually sits. There's no one there. Not even the streetlight shines. The plastic bucket is gone.

I turn to the house to see my cousins' faces pressed against the top-floor window. "Is it okay, Donna, if I sit here?" I call out nice and loud.

She gives me the middle finger.

I slide onto the leather seat and it smells like lemons. I sniff and sniff, searching the air for some remnant of Dray and his bitter-mint-and-sweet-smoke smell—marijuana. But there's nothing but lemons.

"Oh, I got it cleaned before I came here," Kasim says as he presses the button that starts the car. "I know it's not mine and all, so I wanted it to have a different smell, a different feel. All right with you?"

I smile and nod.

He turns on the radio and I brace myself for that heavy bass music. But it's something different. Something like jazz, but still hip-hop. I look at him. He looks at me and smiles. I start moving to the beat a little. He does the same and turns up the volume. The rapper's voice is smooth, as if he's reciting love poems. I've never heard anything like it, and a chill travels up my back, making me smile wider than I probably have in a long time.

"You like that?" he asks.

I nod.

"J Dilla. Detroit legend. He died when I was little. I'm into the classics, but all Detroit, all day. Motown, J Dilla, Slum Village." He pulls the car away from the curb and his voice blends well with the music, as if he's a background rapper for this J Dilla.

"What about Eminem?" I ask.

Kasim laughs. "Slim Shady? What'd you do, watch *8 Mile*

140

before you got here? You need to upgrade your info, Ms. Fabulous. You heard of Big Sean?"

He presses some buttons near the dashboard and the music changes. It's something familiar I've heard on the radio in Chantal's car. Kasim raises the volume and he dances while slowly turning down the corner of Joy Road.

And there is Papa Legba, leaning on his cane with a cigar in his mouth and looking straight into the car with his gleaming white eyes. My skin crawls, and suddenly what was just a smooth hip-hop song now sounds like heavy conga drums—a downbeat rhythm, like for the *Petwo lwas*, the fiery spirits signaling danger ahead. My stomach twists into a knot and I almost want to tell Kasim to stop the car and let me out.

But he reaches over and eases his hand into my hand as we drive past Bad Leg, and my stomach settles, my thoughts calm. And we stay like that for the whole ride down Joy Road, until we reach the highway. Then he drives into downtown, toward Broadway Street, where we reach a wide, brightly lit tall building that's just for cars. We park Dray's car, then walk in the same direction as the other people coming out of nice cars and wearing fancy coats and high-heel shoes. I look over at Kasim and down at my own clothes, and begin to feel very underdressed for whatever this surprise date will be.

We get in line for a theater called the Detroit Opera House. A poster near the entrance has a photo of a lean, muscular dancing black couple and the name ALVIN AILEY. It's a dance performance. Within seconds, everything from the past few weeks that has caused me so much worry melts away like ice in the sun.

"I'm guessing you like dance, seeing how you was trying to do the Detroit Jit back at that party," Kasim says, easing closer to me as the line moves.

I nod because I'm speechless. I've seen live dancers before, at folklore festivals in Port-au-Prince and Les Cayes. And at parties where Haitians dance to *compas* as if they're on *Dancing with the Stars*. But never anyone like the ones on that poster, with legs and arms as long as the sky stretches. And never with such people for an audience—all black people with their faces smiling bright, the sounds of their voices all around us like music. It's as if I'm mingling with the bourgeois businesspeople and entertainers from Petionville. I keep my eyes on one beautiful couple where the woman's hair sits high and round on top of her head like Jesus's halo. She and her man hold hands and kiss and talk and kiss some more.

My eyes are so fixed on them that I jump when Kasim puts his arm around me. Then I realize that we are not as beautiful, I am not as beautiful as that woman. I remember what I have on—jeans, a plain sweatshirt, sneakers, and Pri's oversized coat. I gasp and cross my arms across my chest.

"Kasim, I can't go in there like this," I whisper. "You didn't tell me that I had to dress up."

He looks down at me. "You look good. You got on your

Jordans, some nice tight jeans. If anybody look at you funny, you tell 'em you reppin' the west side."

I roll my eyes. "I'm serious. This is a nice event and I could've worn something nice. You have on good clothes."

"That's 'cause I was trying to impress you, not them. I wanna show you that I could be bougie, too. Remember? Do some bougie shit with my bougie girl."

"Kasim!" I look away from him because I want to go home and change.

"Hey." He turns me around and gets really close to my face. "All that matters is that you're bougie on the inside. You could be from poor-ass Haiti or live in a trailer park, but as long as you have a bougie heart, you can aim for the finer things in life."

He makes his face look very serious, as if he's a professor. His glasses slide to the tip of his nose and he looks out at me from the top of the frames. I laugh and lean into him. He pulls me in and wraps his arms around me. He holds me tighter and kisses the top of my head. I sniff his shirt, then lift my head to take in the bare skin of his neck. It's a mix of sweetness and too-strong cologne. I only move because we're at the front of the line and we have to go inside. When he hands over the two tickets to the usher, I see that they cost over one hundred dollars each.

I forget every single thing in the world, every heartache, every tear, every pain as I watch that performance. The dancers,

the music, the lights, the people in the theater are all so beautiful that I want to wear them on my skin for the rest of my life.
And Manman. If only I can wrap everything that I'm experi-
encing and place it in a box as a gift for her. I would put into the
box the dancers and music and the whole theater as if they are
perfectly wrapped clothes and jewelry. I must bring her here
when she comes.

"How much were the tickets?" I ask Kasim as we're walking
back to the car.

"Excuse me, that's not a polite question, Ms. Fabulous."

"I don't want you to spend so much money on me. You have
your mother, that shitty car, and don't you want to go back to
school? That's what you said."

He laughs a little. "I think it's so cute the way you say
'shitty.'"

"Kasim?"

"All right." He stops in front of Dray's car. "I'm not a baller,
Fabulous. But you're different from a lot of these other girls out
here. I mean, they might make fun of how you talk and all,
but you're more bougie than a whole lot of these girls. And by
bougie, I mean classy shit. Like going to the theater instead of
the movies. My uncle taught me that. To be honest, I got the
tickets from him."

I pull the coat's hood up over my head because the wind is
getting colder and stronger. The headlights from other people's
cars are like the lights on the stage, making everything bright

and then dark over and over again. "Your uncle seems like a nice man."

"Yeah. Well, Q is not my real uncle. He's Dray's uncle, but it's like he's everybody's uncle. Shit. He might even be your uncle."

He opens the car door for me as I let his last words settle in my bones. "My uncle?" I ask when he gets in the car.

"Yeah, Uncle Q. He owns Q over there on West Chicago. That's his club, practically his block. That's where he runs his business. And that's where I first fell in love." He turned to me and smiled extra wide, showing his teeth.

"Why would he be my uncle, too? I had an uncle. My cousins' father."

"Oh, yeah. The legendary Haitian Phil."

"What?"

"Pri won't ever let anybody forget her father. She's always swearing on his grave, right before she gets to stompin' on some girl's face. 'I swear on my father's grave this, I swear on my father's grave that.' And whoever be working for Uncle Q, she won't ever let them forget that it was her father, Haitian Phil, who went down for Q."

"What? Went down for Q?" I ask again. This time I'm staring at him with my eyes wide and my ears even wider.

"Damn, Fabulous. Your cousins don't tell you shit. Good. Stay out of it. West side logic, Detroit politics, as I like to say. I don't fuck with any of that shit. And neither should you."

Maybe this is Papa Legba's doing—making Kasim talk

more than he should. Teaching me about Dray and Q and Uncle Phil. Suddenly I feel caught up in something bigger than myself. If he can tell me what I need to know about Dray, maybe Kasim will finally be the key that will help me pull my mother through to this side.

I don't ask any more questions—instead, right before Kasim pushes the button to start the car, I pull on the sleeve of his coat, lean over, and kiss him on the cheek. He turns to me and I kiss him on the lips. Then he turns his whole body to me, takes my face with both his hands, and kisses me long and deep.

When we drive back to American Street, all the lights look brighter, maybe there are more stars in the sky, and this city is more beautiful than it has ever been.

FIFTEEN

THE LAST FEW nights have been a mix of strange feelings stirring in my belly. I am warm honey when I think of Kasim. And then I become an empty coconut shell without its sweet water and flesh when I think of my mother. Maybe every cell in my body is starting to feel her absence. Even my own hair is longing for her thick fingers in my scalp—the way she would part and grease and braid and hum and tell sad or funny stories. My skin aches for that sizzling midday Port-au-Prince sun when sweat would ease down my forehead and back. Still, there is a sliver of hope now that I am close to the information I need. When my mother comes, she will be the bright midday sun that will warm up these cold days and nights. I can almost feel her presence as morning creeps in through the window and reaches me on the air mattress.

So I stay in bed.

Even as my cousins get ready and tell me over and over again to get up, I stay there.

"Fab, if you don't feel well, I have to call the school so they don't think you're cutting," Chantal says while standing over me.

"My belly hurts," I lie. What I want to say is that my heart hurts for Manman.

"Okay. I'll call the school. But you have to make up the homework. Okay?"

I nod and pull the covers up over my head. I need this day to think and plan.

After my cousins leave for school, I go downstairs to make some tea. This is how Manman and I would plan our next move—over some tea or coffee. All I want is my mother here with me—her voice, her jokes, her cooking, her advice. What would she think of my cousins? What would she and Matant Jo be doing all day together? What would she think of Kasim? What would she say to Donna about her mean boyfriend?

It wasn't supposed to be like this. My mother and I had been so happy, so excited because all our dreams were coming true. We were supposed to all be together—my aunt, my cousins, my mother, and I. And in just a few hours everything changed. Everything.

Back upstairs, I drop my body down onto Chantal's bed, press my face against her pillow, and scream. Drops of anger trickle out, little by little, as if every single setback over these past few weeks has exploded. Tiny bombs escape me. I sob and my body shakes trying to get everything out.

I take Chantal's blanket, wrap it around me, and pretend it's my mother's arms. I rock myself until there is nothing left but my small whimpers. I'm like an infant, slowly sliding into sleep.

Hush, little baby

Don't say a word.

His song travels to the window and gives a gentle knock. I get up and pull the curtain back. His overturned plastic bucket is there. His songs return.

Papa's gonna release

Your little jailbird.

I throw on some clothes, grab a coat, and rush outside. I slow down as I get closer. There's something different about him. His left leg is still limp in front of him, the cane is leaning against the lamppost, and, again, he has a cigar in his hand. I watch for the dancing smoke, but the cigar isn't lit like it was the night of my date with Kasim on Saturday. Nor is the streetlight. It's daytime. This is the first time I've seen Papa Legba when the sun is high in the sky.

"You are early," I say.

Just an early bird

Bringing the word.

"What's the word, Papa Legba?"

Word on the streets,

Or word on the beat?

"Street? Beat? What? You always have tricks, eh, Legba?"

Word on the street is word on the block

Word on the block is word in that house

Word in that house is word on that door

Word on that door is word on his soul

Word on his soul is word on my tomb

Word on my tomb does not spell doom.

With that last verse, Papa Legba's cigar lights up, the street-light buzzes, and as if God suddenly threw a blanket over this part of Detroit, a heavy cloud blocks the sun and it becomes dark. Thunder rolls across the sky and I look down, not up, because I've heard this sound before.

I was only a little girl when my home was almost split in half. And while everyone around me thought the sky was coming apart right above our heads, it was the ground that was surrendering under the weight of our heavy burdens. And maybe this corner of American and Joy is collapsing under the weight of all that troubles me, too—we left everything we loved behind in Haiti and my mother was put into something like jail. And now, a detective has asked me to sacrifice a bad guy so my mother can be free. Sacrifice. We cannot get something for nothing, Manman always says. Prayers, songs, and offerings are not enough. We have to meet God halfway. So I know what I must do.

Heavy raindrops begin to pound on my head like drums, and when I look up, Bad Leg is gone. Papa Legba's words were *street, block, house, door, soul, tomb,* and *doom.* I pause on the word *block.* I've heard Kasim say it before—*block.* I didn't know if he meant a block of ice, or a cinder block, but he said *block* and that an Uncle Q owns it. Along with that club.

I step away from the house. I have to go find this block, this street, this house, this door to the club, to this underworld where Dray resides. I pull the hood of my coat up over my head, and it's thick enough to keep the rainwater away from my hair. My Jordans are getting muddy, and if Pri sees them like this, she will fight me. She cleans hers with a toothbrush every night, even though she wears a different pair the next day.

I keep walking, and when I look to the left, Papa Legba is standing there on the corner of Dover and American, leaning on his cane with rain dripping from the brim of his hat. Behind him is a white house with Christmas decorations, even though it's only November. He looks strange, as if he's just a visitor in this world. I wait for a car to pass before crossing the street, and by the time I reach the other corner, Papa Legba is gone.

The rain is lighter now, so I quickly walk past the houses to reach the other corner. But this part of American Street stretches long. I pass house after house, empty lot after empty lot. Most homes look as if they have families who love them; others look like abandoned orphans with their burned-out roofs and missing windows. A few dogs bark and I jump. An old man calls out, so I walk faster. A car slows down next to me, so I pretend to wave to someone in the distance. The car drives away. And that's when he appears again. I can see him all the way at the end of the sidewalk.

He stands in front of a house. My heart jumps because maybe this is it. This is the house with the door with the soul with the tomb that doesn't spell doom. But as I examine the front gate leading to the house, Papa Legba disappears again. This *lwa* is full of tricks. There is nothing about the house that gives me a sign or clue, so I keep walking. Maybe Papa Legba will appear at the same corner again, telling me to come back and make another turn, or enter that house. I keep looking back, but he's not there. It's his way of saying that I am close, that I don't need his help anymore. So I keep going. Now I have to find this place that will lead me to Dray without Papa Legba's help.

I step over old railroad tracks and continue to walk down one more stretch of American Street. There aren't as many houses as before, and finally, I see West Chicago. I turn left toward the church called House of Canaan, and the club on the other corner is now as clear as the sun behind the parting clouds.

I remember that bright-purple door on the short and wide gray building that takes up the whole section of this street. This is the block, I realize. And there is the letter *Q*, drawn in shiny, silver paint. *Street, block, house, door* echo in my mind again.

I pull on the door handle and a dog starts to bark. I jump and step away from the door. Another dog joins in. Two dogs barking. I want to run back, but I stand still. I've come this far.

"Ay yo, Fabulous!" someone calls out.

My whole body tingles and I freeze. I close my eyes to utter Papa Legba's name for help because I recognize that voice. I see Dray holding two dogs on short leashes. Angry dogs. Dogs that look as if they want to tear me apart.

"What you doing here, Fabulous?" he says, still with that eye patch, like Baron Samedi. He's standing by the door near the side of the building, a secret passageway, maybe. The tomb.

At the same moment, the purple door opens, and a fat guy I recognize stands at the entrance. He was there at that party patting down the people coming in and keeping others out.

There is no Papa Legba here to guide my steps. I'm here on the street, on the block, at the house, by the door. . . .

"I asked you a question, Fabulous. What? You looking for Kasim or something?" His words don't glide out of his mouth—they pulse.

"Q" is all I say. Then I want to take it back.

The fat man by the door shifts his weight. He steps out of the entrance and lets the door shut behind him. My stomach drops. The dogs are still barking.

"What about Q?" Dray asks, cocking his head to one side.

"This is the name of the club, right? I remember coming here for a party." My hands are sweating; my body itches.

"Get the fuck in here," Dray says, motioning with his head for me to follow him in as the fat man comes to take the dogs away. He pulls their leashes and they whimper.

The house. The door. The soul. Then it settles on me like falling concrete. This is also Papa Legba's doing. The door is open. So I must take it from here. I walk past the barking dogs and the fat man, past Dray, and into this building.

It's dark in the back of the club. A single long table is in the middle of the room with about six metal folding chairs around it. One lightbulb hangs from a long cord and swings a little after Dray pulls the door closed. It slams and I breathe in and out slowly, licking my lips and looking every which way, searching for words, ideas, anything. How can I get the information I need? I say, "My mother is coming soon. She was in jail."

"Oh, yeah?" He crosses his arms over his chest and spreads his legs. "Your moms? In jail? Where, Haiti?"

I relax a bit because I'm telling the truth. "No, here. In New Jersey. A detention center. But she's coming soon. I want to throw her a party. Here. This is a nice place."

He laughs. "Oh, that's real cute. Your cousins threw Jo a party here when she turned forty, I think. Matter of fact, it was my uncle Q who organized the whole thing."

"Uncle Q?"

"Yeah. Maybe I should introduce you. . . . Better yet, you'll meet him soon enough if you and Kasim are serious like that."

I nod.

"Y'all serious like that? 'Cause you and him could have what me and Donna have."

"But you hurt her," I say without thinking.

He laughs again. "She hurts me, too. She breaks my fucking heart every day. Now, I don't want you doing that shit to my boy Kasim. Feel me?"

I don't say anything. I don't move.

"Feel me, *Fabulous*?"

I nod slowly.

"Now, let your cousins handle that party shit. Don't let me catch you snooping around here. Kasim wouldn't want anything to happen to you," he says with a half smile.

"Ay yo, Dray!" someone calls out from the front.

The dogs start barking again. Dray goes over to the far end of the room and pulls something out of the drawer of a filing cabinet. My eyes are glued to it, to how he's holding it. And it's not until he's just a few inches from me that I see it's a gun. I can't take my eyes off it.

"Come here," he says.

He has a gun. I don't move one inch.

"I said come here!" His words are like ice—cold and stinging.

I do move. But not my feet. I sway forward a little bit. My mind wants to obey his command, but my body is afraid of what will happen if I go over to him.

"Dray, man!" someone calls out again.

He holds the gun up toward the ceiling, his elbow bent. The dogs bark louder. Voices filter in from outside the club. "Don't leave," he says, and walks out of the back room.

The door doesn't click all the way shut and a sliver of sunlight seeps in. Again, a door has opened for me. But this time, I'm sure it's to get out.

As I run back home, my heart leaps out of my chest, my head pounds, and I almost collapse on the front steps. I take a minute to catch my breath, then pull out my phone and look at Detective Stevens's number. I don't wait for her to call. This time I call.

"Hello. This is Fabiola."

"Yes, I know," she says. "How are you?"

"Dray's uncle is a guy named Q." My breathing is still heavy. I can't get the words out fast enough. "My uncle Phillip went down for him, or something like that."

"You sound out of breath. Are you okay? Did something just happen?"

"Q runs a business out of that club. Dray is there. And . . . there is a gun."

"We know about the club, Fabiola. We need something that places Dray and his drugs at that party in Grosse Point. I need you to calm down a bit so you can understand what I'm saying."

"But . . . ," I start to say. I take in a deep breath. "He is doing bad things in that place."

She's quiet for a moment. Then she says, "Thank you, Fabiola. You're doing good, but I want you to be very careful. Don't put yourself in any dangerous situations. Just listen and pay close attention. Get me something I can use."

I nod, but she can't see me, of course.

"Fabiola?"

"Yes?"

"If you can be free tomorrow around noon, I can arrange a phone call with your mother."

I close my eyes and exhale. I don't say a word to her. She lets me have this moment of quiet gratitude and hangs up the phone.

It starts to rain hard again. I let it pour over my head for a few minutes before I go back inside.

SIXTEEN

WE'RE NOT ALLOWED to have our cell phones in class. But at school the next day, I manage to keep mine in my book bag all morning. After every class, I run into the bathroom to see if the detective has left a number or has called.

Then, around eleven thirty in the morning, after my math class, the detective sends a text with a time. My mother has my number. She will be calling exactly at noon. Good. It'll be lunchtime, so I won't have to miss a class. I'm in a bathroom stall and I press myself against the door, holding the phone to my heart. I count the minutes, the seconds, the milliseconds until my phone rings.

"*Alo, alo? Manman?*"

"*Alo?*"

"Manman?"

"Fabiola? Oh, Faboubou!"

"Manman! *Kommen ou ye?* How are you?"

"Oh, *mezanmi*! Fabiola? When can I see your face, dear daughter?"

"Manman, I'm working so hard to get you out. I promise. We will see each other soon. How are they treating you? What are you eating? It's so cold. Are you warm, Manman? Do you have enough clothes? Do you have socks? Do they give you soap?"

"No, Fab. How are *you*? I don't want you to worry about me. How are your cousins, and my dear sister? How is school? Fab, tell me that you are studying lots."

"*Wi*, Manman. Yes, yes, yes! I'm working to get you out. Get your things ready. I have your suitcases here. I will pick out a dress for you to wear when you arrive."

"I tell you don't worry about me. That is Marjorie's job. Now, where is she? Is she sending money? She needs to send me a good lawyer and money. Is she coming to see me?"

"No, Manman. I'm taking care of it."

"Stay out of it, Fabiola. Focus on your books. Let me speak to Marjorie."

"Matant Jo is not here. I will tell her— *Alo? Alo?*"

"*Alo?* Fabiola?"

"Manman, I can't hear you. *Alo?*"

"*Alo? Alo?*"

"Manman? I'm here. I'm here. *Alo, alo?* What happened? I can't hear you. Hello? Manman, I love you. I love you! Hello?"

Someone knocks on the stall's door.

"Fabiola? Who are you talking to?" It's Imani.

I need to think quick, because this little slice of happiness is part of a secret deal. "Just my aunt," I lie.

"Well, you need to put that phone away so you don't get detention," she says.

I hold the phone in my hand even as I walk out of the bathroom. Detention or not, I just spoke to my mother and there is sunshine again.

I've been knocking for almost two minutes with no answer, so I open the door. "Matant," I start to say when I see her lying on her bed. But before I even ask my question, she reaches over the edge of her bed, picks something up, and throws it straight at me. I don't even have time to duck. It hits the wall next to the door and lands right at to my feet. A slipper. My aunt threw a slipper at me. I quickly close the door.

"Hey, hey!" she calls out. "Come back in here! You wake me up and then you're gonna leave just like that?"

I open the door again. Slowly this time, ready to duck. I don't step all the way in.

"What do you want?" she yells. "Come in here and close the door behind you."

I do as she says. "*Wi*, Matant."

"I keep telling you, *English*. Now, what do you want?" Her voice is softer. She rolls to her back. It's dark in her room, and the one window behind her headboard is covered with a thick curtain. The air is thick, too, a mix of alcohol and food. Her bedroom is next to the kitchen.

"I spoke to my mother today," I say soft, soft, as if my words are tiptoeing.

"What? How did you find her?"

I pause for a long while. "There was a number on the website. I just gave them her name," I lie. "She wanted to speak to you. She really wanted to hear your voice."

"That easy, eh?" she says, slowly sitting up. She yawns and rubs her face. It's as if sleeping makes her tired. "So what is her situation? Why are they keeping her there? How is she doing?"

"I think she is okay."

Her hair is smashed in the back and it fans out around her head like a peacock's, but not as beautiful. "She did it to herself, you know. She's always been so hardheaded, that Valerie. Just like me," she says, and scratches her head with both hands. "Well, I am so happy you spoke with her. She will take good care of herself. My hands are tied, Fabiola."

Her words are small and sad, even though she now knows that her sister is okay.

"Aunt Jo, why do you sleep so much?" I ask.

She inhales long and deep. Then she coughs. "Get me some water."

In a less than a minute, I'm by her bed, placing the glass of cool water on her nightstand. She quickly drinks it and her gulps are loud and deep. "Do you want more?"

"No, I'm good," she says. She inhales again. "No, really. Thank you." She's looking straight at me now.

"You're welcome."

"You've done more for me in these past few weeks than my own daughters have."

I shake my head, wanting to reject the compliment.

"No, really. I mean, you cook, you clean. I've never seen the stove so spotless, the refrigerator so . . . organized," she says.

I look around the room, and I want to clean up in here, too. There are a few clothes on the floor next to her bed. But I want to throw out the things on her nightstand most of all. The drinking glasses I've been looking for all week are there. And bottles and bottles of pills. But I've never seen her go to the doctor or the hospital.

"Where do you feel pain?" I finally ask. "Is it your heart, your back, your bones, your head?"

She closes her eyes. "Everywhere, Fabiola. Everywhere."

"But you're too young, Matant. I mean, Aunt."

"Tell me about my sister. Was she in pain, too? Because whenever I called her, she would say everything is fine. Just fine. I never believed her."

"She wasn't in pain, but she was tired of fighting. Everything about Port-au-Prince was a fight."

"Didn't I send you enough money?"

"Yes, of course. But . . ."

"But, I know," she said. "Money can't buy happiness, as they say. I should know."

Silence falls between us, but before it spreads and pushes us further apart, I take her hand in mine.

She looks up at me. "So, what is your plan?"

"To get my mother home." I don't think that's what she was asking. Maybe she wants to hear that I am going to be a doctor like Chantal. But I tell her the truth. First, my mother. Then, everything else.

I glide my finger along the top of the dresser next to me and collect a thick layer of dust. "I am not tired of fighting. I am just starting," I say.

"Oh, yeah?" She laughs. "Tell me, what is it that you're fighting, Faboubou?"

My heart wants to collapse because she says my nickname exactly the way my mother says it, with the same voice. *Faboubou.*

"Matant. If you call me that, then I will call you Matant. That's how I've always known you. When you used to phone Haiti, I would say Matant Jo. You never corrected me then."

"You're in America now, Fabiola. You have to practice your English."

"I know my English."

"Thanks to me."

"If my mother was here, you would do the same thing to her? Make her call you *Jo*?"

"Of course." She comes over to the dresser, opens a drawer, and pulls out a pair of underwear. Then she undresses right in front me. I don't turn away. I examine her body. It looks swollen, as if every sad thing in the world has stuck to her bones. She has a hard time pulling off the nightgown from the left side of her body. So I help her.

I place the nightgown over my arm and start picking up the other clothes from the floor. A bunch of empty pill bottles and a few alcohol bottles lie open on their sides. I pick those up, too. I look around for a trash can, but there isn't one. So I hold in my arms and hands as many of her dirty clothes and pill bottles and alcohol bottles as I can.

She's sitting at the edge of her bed buttoning her shirt. She tries to smooth down her hair, but it still sticks up. So I set down the things on the dresser, grab a comb from her nightstand, and help her with her hair, just like the many times I've done it for my mother and Pri. My aunt melts beneath my hands. Her good shoulder hunches over, she lets out a deep quiet breath, and before long, she starts humming. It's a song I know, a song my mother sings, too. So I hum with her.

Then she asks, "Did everyone respect my sister? She was a big-time *mambo*, right?"

"Yes and no. And no and yes," I say as I kneel behind her

on the bed, parting the thin, graying strands of her hair. I can't help but think that my own mother's hair is still full and black.

"What is that, a trick answer? I did not ask you a trick question. Your mother was right. You are Legba's child."

"He's at the corner, Matant. He watches over this house, you know."

"Who? Bad Leg? That crazy crackhead?" She laughs and sounds just like Pri.

"Chantal said you used to call him Legba, too. You knew."

"I didn't know shit, just like you don't know shit, Faboubou. Don't worry. You'll learn."

I stop braiding her hair. "That's not true, Matant Jo," I say, trying to make my English sound like my cousins'. "I know things. Me and my mother, we did well in Haiti, with or without your money."

She laughs her Pri laugh again, but only the right side of her body shakes. "You did well in Haiti *with* my money. You think I was going to let my sister rot in the countryside with a new baby in her hands?"

"We prayed for you. When I was a young girl and I couldn't even understand anything, I knew that it was my job to pray for my aunt and cousins because it was the only reason my papers said that I am American. We were grateful for that, not just for the money."

"When you were born, I told your mother to stay. Why did she have to leave, eh? When it was time for her to go, I tore up her ticket. Why would I send my sister back to that country with a baby girl and no father, no family?" She turns halfway around, but she doesn't look at me. She stares at the wall. "It's her fault, you know. She should've stayed."

"But Matant, she's not stuck in Haiti. She's stuck in a jail, in a place called New Jersey. How is that her fault? She wanted to come here to be with you. She knew you were sick. All that coughing, and you were complaining that the twins were out of control. She was coming to help."

"No. She finally came to her senses, that's what." She slowly gets up from the bed. It's as if every move she makes hurts her body.

"I'm not done yet," I say, still with the comb in my hand. Only half her head is in braids.

"Yes, you are."

"Matant Jo," I say. "Bad Leg at the corner, he's not just a crazy man. He is Papa Legba and he is opening doors and big, big gates. I will show you. I promise."

She turns to me. "Child, this is Detroit. Ain't no *Papa Legba* hanging out on corners. Only dealers and junkies. You don't know shit. But don't worry. You'll figure it out."

My whole body sinks onto her bed, still with her comb in my hand and with the scent of cigarette smoke, alcohol, sweat, pain, and grief on the tips of my fingers.

MARJORIE & VALERIE'S STORY

When I was fifteen and my little sister was thirteen, a whole new world opened up to us. Not in the way that the world opened up to Chantal when a fancy private high school offered her a full scholarship. Not in the way that Princess put all her dresses and skirts into trash bags and started dressing like the son I never had. And not in the way that the world opened up to Primadonna when she threatened to run away with her new boyfriend if I didn't let her go on dates with him.

Our world opened up because a long-time dictator was thrown out of Haiti. This dictator was the heavy boot on our skinny necks. Our dear parents in heaven never knew a world without Jean-Claude "Baby Doc" Duvalier and his father, François Duvalier. We thought there would be freedom and democracy, and that money would start flowing into the country like a long-awaited rainstorm.

But when the dictator and his fancy wife left, everything broke. There was no order, no peace.

But as thirteen- and fifteen-year-old girls, with no mother and father to watch over us, our bodies were like poor countries—there was always a dictator trying to rule over us.

We were hired to work in the house of a well-known business-man. And he would watch us while we worked. We let him look. Eyes are only dull blades, but hands are as sharp as broken glass. Eventually, he touched me, and I was cut. That day, I screamed for my sister. She then screamed for his wife.

We had to leave his house that night. We wanted to leave the whole country.

Valerie and I joined the crowds that gathered by the shores of Cité Soleil waiting for a boat to Miami. We gave our money to the captain—a skinny fisherman with missing teeth. We folded our-selves between a woman with too many bags and a man holding a crying baby. Valerie offered to hold the baby when the waters got too rough. The woman had to throw her bags overboard when water started to fill the boat. Our precious things were soaked, and there were cries and screams. Everyone cursed and prayed and shouted as our legs became wet and cold.

We were too heavy. Not with our bags. Not with our bodies. But with our burdens.

The captain yelled for some of us to get off. But we couldn't simply walk away—we were surrounded by water. We huddled together because the boat was sinking.

Valerie and I never let go of each other. She whispered La Siren's name over and over again, praying for the beautiful mermaid to rise up from the depths of the ocean and save us.

So the spirit of La Siren came in the form of a big boat, with strong arms to pull us up and over the side of the metal railing.

We had not drowned in that ocean. For me, it was so that I could find love and freedom in this new home called America with my beautiful girls. And for Valerie . . . if she did not perish in that ocean, then there is more for her to do in this life. We are still here.

SEVENTEEN

"**YOU WERE ABSENT.** I wanted to give you back your paper," Mr. Nolan says as he hands me a folder with my name on it.

I look down at my revised paper about Toussaint L'Ouverture. There's now an A at the top. There are no red marks on my carefully chosen words and sentences and quotes from books on Chantal's shelves and from the internet. I listened to Imani and "gave textual evidence." It worked.

"How are you adjusting to Detroit?" he asks. His brows are furrowed as if he expects me to give him some bad news. His beard and mustache are so thick that I can't tell whether he smiles or not.

He sits there, waiting for an answer, but I don't know where to begin.

Finally, he exhales and nods. "I know. It's an adjustment," he says. "If you ever want to write about what it's like for you, being from Haiti and all, you certainly can. I will count it as extra credit. And it wouldn't have to be a research paper."

"How are *you* adjusting to Detroit?" I finally ask him. My question makes no sense because he lives here. He is not new to this city, to this country. He is only the second black man teacher I've had in my life—even in Haiti—so I want to know what his life is like here, if he has a wife and children and a big house. Knowing this bit of an American story will help me to dream a little bit.

He chuckles. "I've adjusted just fine. Had no choice. Detroit born and raised. Went to school. Messed up a couple of times. But got back up and did what I had to do. So I expect no less from you, or any of my students. I'm here to help."

He doesn't really give me the answer that I want, so I only smile, thank him, and gather my things. Before I leave the classroom, Mr. Nolan calls my name again.

"You're doing very well, Fabiola. Stay focused," he says with what I think is a smile hidden beneath all that beard.

"I will" is all I say.

I let Imani see my paper while we walk through the lobby out of the building.

"He was easy on you," she says.

"What? No way. I worked so hard," I reply as I zip up my coat.

"Yeah, right. When did you find the time to work on that paper? Last thing I heard was Kasim taking you to the opera house to see Alvin Ailey. That's some real fancy shit." She looks me up and down as if I'm dirty.

"What are you saying, Imani?" I shove her a little and try not to smile.

"What'd you put out for him to spend money on you like that?" She laughs.

I shove her harder and she almost stumbles down the school's front steps. "I didn't do anything with him."

"Well, he's sure expecting something back." She laughs hard while holding on to the handrail. "And when you do give it up, he's gonna be hitting all the walls!" She pushes her pelvis back and forth.

"Oh, Imani! That is nasty," I say, trying really hard to keep from laughing.

"Is that what you want Dray to do to you?" Donna's voice cuts through Imani's laugh. She's standing at the top of the concrete steps. Imani wipes the smile from her face and glances at me.

"Don't you look at her," Donna says, coming down a couple of steps. "Do you like him?"

I touch Donna's shoulder. "No, she doesn't like Dray," I answer for Imani.

"That's not what I heard." She gets real close to Imani's face. I get ready to pull Donna away if she tries anything. "You don't want to mess with Dray, trust me. He'll fuck your whole shit up, *Imani*. And don't think I'm saying this 'cause I'm jealous. I'm just trying to look out for you." She continues down the stairs but keeps her eyes on Imani.

"She's not gonna do anything to you," I say loud enough for Donna to hear. "She just thinks Dray likes you."

Imani stares straight at me. "You're real dumb, Fabiola. You don't know shit. Your cousins will drag me out here on these streets. And it's all 'cause I'm hanging with you."

"No. Donna is jealous, that's all. Pri and Chantal don't have a problem with you."

"They will if Donna ever put a hand on me. I got cousins, too, you know."

I try to hold her arm, to stop her from leaving, but Chantal is honking the car horn at the curb, and this time I have to choose blood over water.

Once we're all in the car, I say, "Donna, Imani helped me with my paper. She's not trying to steal your boyfriend."

"I know" is all she says.

"Then why are you making her so scared?"

"'Cause that's what we do, Fabulous," Pri answers for her. "That's just how the Three Bees roll."

I'm quiet for a moment, then ask, "But why? Why do you have to be so mean?"

"I don't want her to even think she has a chance with Dray," Donna says.

"But she doesn't," I say.

"And I need to let her know that. Some of these girls out here will drop their panties for a nigga like Dray—thinking that he'll buy them shit and that he really loves them."

Pri makes a fake coughing sound. "You might want to check that mirror, D," she says.

"Shut up, Pri! I can handle Dray. Your friend Imani, she'll get burned real bad if she's not careful. I'm just looking out for her."

"So why don't you just tell her that instead of being so nasty to her?" I say.

"Damn it, Fabiola!" Chantal finally speaks. "'Cause they will mess with you. That's why. The same way they messed with me back then. If these girls think you're scared and that you're not gonna fight back, they will mess with you. And you don't want none of that. Trust me. And because we do what we do, they won't bother you, so you can just worry about your school-work and your essay. Okay?"

I nod. I understand. They are the Three Bees. They not only have to protect their bodies, but they have to protect their name and their story. And if they are my cousins, my family, I have to help protect them, too. But I have to do the same for my friends, too, like Imani.

We drive until we reach a big house with a bunch of girls standing outside. Donna is the first to open her door.

"She's not gonna want to," Chantal says.

Donna stares me down through the window. "Let's go, Fab. You're getting your nails done, your hair did . . ."

"What?" I say, looking toward the house. That's when I see the sign that reads UNIQUE HAIR ESSENTIALS.

"Come on. Dray's picking us up at ten," Donna says. "It's his birthday."

My insides sink to the bottom of the deepest, darkest place here. "But I don't want to do anything to my hair."

Donna sighs. "Kasim really likes you. Dray said he ain't never seen him act like that for no girl. So, you coming out with us tonight. You, Kasim, me, and Dray. But you are definitely not rolling with us looking like that. Let's go."

She starts walking to the house without looking back to see if I am following her. I'm still in the backseat.

"You don't have to go if you don't want to. Especially if Dray is paying for everything," Chantal says.

"What?" I say.

"Dray is paying for you to look good while you roll with him, his boy, and his girl. That's how he do. He tried to pull that shit with me and Pri. I gave him back his money. So you don't have to go in with Donna. Kasim will still like you."

Pri shakes her head. "I'm not down for none of this shit, Fab. Sometimes I don't even want you to be with Kasim 'cause he's Dray's boy."

"If you and Chantal don't like Dray, then why is he still in your lives?" I ask.

"'Cause of Donna. She doesn't just like him. She *loves* him. So it's on you. This'll really be for Donna," Pri says.

"For Donna? Then I'll go." I scoot out of the car taking my bag with me.

I'm tired of hearing about Dray, talking about Dray, and seeing Dray. I have a chance to hand him over to that detective, and this opportunity is sunshine after a thunderstorm. Stevens said that the club was a good start, but she needed more information that will put Dray and his drugs at that party in Grosse Pointe. I have to be like Papa Legba now—a trickster. So I will wear the costume, say the right things, and play the game to get what I need.

The girls outside the house don't even look my way. Some come over to Donna and kiss her on both cheeks. A lady comes out of the house with long flaming-red hair and wearing enough makeup for a whole beauty contest. She is so tall that the top of her head brushes against a nearby tree branch. My eyes are glued to her tight purple dress that sparkles in the late-afternoon sun under her light-brown fur coat. She looks like jewelry, or something that belongs in a store window. She must be a mannequin.

"Hey, Miss Sandra!" Donna calls out, and goes over to hug the mannequin.

"Hey, baby girl!" the lady shouts back in a deep, booming voice, catching me off guard.

I have never seen something so beautiful and strange. I stare at Miss Sandra from the top of her head to her feet. She has on the same black high-heel boots as Donna. They go over her knees and reach up to her thighs.

"You look like you just seen a *haint*!" Miss Sandra says, with her voice like the bottom of the ocean. "Come on! You need a fairy godmother to work some magic on you, honey."

Inside the Unique Hair Essentials house, there are more fancy ladies. Some with hair as long as their legs, others with eyelashes as long as their fingers. A short lady comes over to Donna and gives her a big hug. Then she pushes my cousin, taking me in.

"Let me see what kinda science project you done dragged up in here," she says. Her voice is not as deep, but her slim arms are all hard, tight muscle.

I smile on the inside because I've seen this before in Haiti. This place is like a whole peristyle devoted to the children of Ezili. Posters of beautiful women with hair in all sorts of styles cover the walls. There's a whole table just for plastic heads and their many, many wigs; hair dryers; bins filled with hair rollers of all colors and sizes; shelves lined with nail polish that look like an *arc-en-ciel*, a rainbow; a dress rack full of bright, sparkling clothes.

"Hello, Ms. Science Project!" the lady says, holding out a hand to me. It's soft, soft, as if she's never scrubbed a pot. "I'm Ms. Unique, and this is my laboratory."

"My name is Fabiola," I say, still looking around at the other women, who are all much more than just women.

"Oh, *Fabulous*! I like her already." She turns to Donna. "Your family sure knows how to pick those names, *Primadonna*."

Unique walks away, twitching her small, muscular butt. Donna is already seated on a salon chair, and in front of her is a huge mirror with bright lights all around it and a table covered with all kinds of hair tools, makeup, perfume, and even glass bowls filled with candy. This is a makeshift altar for Ezili with all the things she loves in the world. My whole body tingles when I realize what's happening.

Again, Papa Legba has opened another door. How could I have missed this? Of course, I need Ezili's help, too. And she'd been right under my nose, working through Donna with all her talk about hair, jewelry, clothes, and beauty.

This is what Dray likes. This is why he's with her. This is how I will get to him, too.

"Oooh, honey. What happened?" Unique says, and I quickly get up to see why she's examining Donna's face so closely.

Before Donna covers the left side of her face again with her fake hair, I see the swollen scratch marks. I hadn't noticed how her wigs have been much thicker recently, how she's let the hair fall to her face so that only her eyes, nose, and lips show.

"Oh, no, no, no! Come on, Donna. Let's see it." Unique tries to pull Donna's hand away. "Miss Sandra, come see this baby girl's face."

"Shit! Again, Donna?" Miss Sandra calls out. Two other

women gather around Donna and I try to see her through the mirror, but they all block me.

"I will cut him for you, just say the word, D," Unique says.

"Yes!" I call out. "Yes! That's what Ezili-Danto would do."

They all turn to me and say, "Who?"

I squeeze my way past them to get to Donna. Her wig is off and the scars are as clear as day. My heart sinks when I see how Dray has hurt my dear cousin. "Ezili-Danto, the *lwa* of vengeance for women. She has the scars on her face, too. And she carries a knife. She will cut a man or woman if she feels betrayed."

"I hear that," someone says.

"Yeah, well, I ain't stabbing my man with no dagger," Donna says.

The women talk over her and all I can think is *Don't worry, Donna. I will do it for you.*

When it's my turn on the chair, I let Unique add lots of fake hair to my head. It falls down to my elbows and it tickles the back of my neck. She tweezes my eyebrows and adds fake eyelashes, too. Already, I feel transformed.

I will wear the costume. I will say the right things. I will play the game. I will get Dray.

EIGHTEEN

AFTER UNIQUE DROPS us off, Donna rushes out of the car and
bursts into the house, yelling, "I won, bitches!"

She opens the door wide to make way for my grand entrance.
But Pri and Chantal are not in the living room—it's Matant
Jo and the four men who were here weeks ago. One of them is
counting a pile of cash on the coffee table. Deep in concentra-
tion, he doesn't even look up.

"Oh, nice," Matant Jo says in her deep voice. "Donna's trying to make you her Barbie doll?"

Pri and Chantal hear the shouting and come down—one
shaking her head, the other with her mouth open.

Donna pulls me up the stairs and into her bedroom, where
it's a frenzy of finding the right outfit for my very new hair

and my very new face. Again, I put on a dress, pose for pictures, change into jeans, pose for more pictures. And finally, I'm settled in a pair of tight black pants and an even tighter denim shirt that makes my breasts look much bigger than they really are.

I don't argue with Donna. I let her win. Because tonight, I will be the Ezili-Danto that she is too afraid to be.

We hear the heavy bass from Dray's car outside, and Donna changes her outfit for the twentieth time. It's Dray's birthday, she tells me again. She has to look perfect.

Before we leave, Chantal grabs my arm and says, "Don't change, Fabiola. Be yourself. You don't have to do none of this."

I smile, nod, and follow Donna to Dray's car. Kasim is there waiting, too.

He doesn't smile when he sees me. He looks confused. He doesn't hug me or kiss me; he just stares at my very long fake hair, my long eyelashes, my too-red lipstick, and my perfect eyebrows.

I kiss him, take his hand, and ease into the dark space of the car.

The building where Dray's having his party is like a giant *Petwo* drum that pulses with a heavy rhythm. I feel like I have entered the underworld.

"What's up with that new weave?" Kasim asks as he takes my hand.

"Do you like it?" I ask, gently tossing the hair over my shoulder like I've seen Donna do many times.

"No" is all he says. "But I like you."

I feel so bad that Kasim is confused by the new me, but I'm not here for him. Not tonight.

"Don't let Detroit change you," Kasim says into my ear. His warm breath against my face makes my whole body tingle. "I know you're not used to this. If you wanna leave, just say the word."

I shake my head and gently push him away.

A large group of people greet Dray in all different ways—girls kiss him on the cheek, guys slap his hand and hug him with one arm.

This party is different from the one at Q's club. The beat changes and everyone raises their hand and starts swaying to the music. Kasim starts to recite the words and I wish I knew the words, too.

Dray looks my way and our eyes meet. Kasim puts his arm around me and pulls me in close while we walk toward Dray and Donna.

"You look good, cuzz. Finally. I'm glad you came to your senses," Donna says to me as I reach her side.

I lean in toward her. "Kasim doesn't like it, but all the other boys do," I say as I keep my eyes on Dray. He looks at me again. This time, he smiles and winks because Donna is turned away from him.

"Kasim is nice and all, but honestly, he's a cornball," Donna says.

Dray doesn't take his eyes off me.

"I like him. He's nice" is all I say. Then Kasim goes over to stand next to Dray, and he looks at me, too.

I quickly turn away, afraid to see any hurt in Kasim's eyes. I almost don't want to be with him here; I'm in battle. There's no room for love in this war.

Then I recognize the fat guy from the doorway at Q's. He approaches Dray and says something in his ear. My heart skips because Dray changes. He looks around, shifts his weight from foot to foot, pounds a fist into his palm. I nudge Donna, who keeps her eyes on what's going on, too.

Dray comes toward us. He digs into his pocket and pulls out his keys and phone and hands them to Donna. He kisses her on the cheek. Kasim steps over to me, smiling.

"You gonna be all right?" he asks.

"Where are you going?"

"I'll be right back. Just gotta take care of these dudes trying to start shit in the front." He gives my hand a squeeze before he walks away.

Donna puts Dray's keys in her purse and fidgets with his phone as she leads me to the bathroom.

The music is muted in here. I can finally breathe a little. In the mirror, I look more like Donna's twin than Pri. Unique gave us the same hairstyle, and our faces are similar with our deep-set eyes and high cheekbones. Donna leans against the wall, still playing with Dray's phone.

"Why did he give you his phone, anyway?" I ask.

She puts the phone and her purse down near the sink. "If Kasim ever gives you his phone to hold for him, then you'll know it's legit."

When she goes into the stall, I grab the phone and slide the home screen open before it locks. I glance into the mirror to watch Donna's feet underneath the door. Someone comes in, but I ignore her. I check Dray's messages and scroll up really fast. I see the word *Ka* and know that it's Kasim. I scan the messages that say: *Come thru. Where you at? What's good? Got it. The spot.* And once, *Fab. She cool.*

Donna starts peeing. I scroll down until I find a set of numbers instead of a name. I click on the message: *Come thru the spot on Anderdon on the east side tomorrow. Be ready with my shit.*

Donna is pulling up her pants. The phone buzzes and a new text comes in: *You letting them niggas in son?*

Donna flushes the toilet and I quickly turn off the screen and put the phone back on the counter.

"Did some bitch just text him?" she asks as she washes her hands.

I shrug.

She takes his phone and checks the text.

"Do you think he's cheating on you?" I ask.

She dries her hands, sighs, and says, "No."

I go into one of the stalls, shut the door, pull out my phone, and text Detective Stevens: *Something is happening tomorrow on Anderdon on the east side.*

It's proof. This is what I need to get my manman home.

Kasim is standing by the bathroom door when I come out. He kisses me on the cheek and leans in to say, "Come on. We got a VIP booth. I wanna toast Dray and then we could bounce. I can tell this ain't your vibe. Dray said I could take his car."

The VIP booth is lined with red and blue lightbulbs. Donna sits down next to Dray on a long narrow couch. Other girls surround them, too, but Donna doesn't seem to care. In front of them is a small table holding a big birthday cake. It's Dray's twenty-first birthday. He's holding a bottle in one hand and a glass in the other. Dray stares at me for a long minute before he offers the glass to me.

"Fabulous, come here," he says.

I walk over to him and take the glass.

He picks up another glass and offers it to Kasim. Soon, we're both standing around Dray, his cake, his girls, and his boys raising our glasses of champagne.

"I wanna shout out my man Kasim," Dray says over the music. "I think he found the one."

Kasim puts his arm around me and kisses me on the cheek. But out of the corner of my eye, I can tell that Dray keeps looking at me as he sips his champagne. I don't drink any of it.

Instead, I place the full glass on the table next to Dray's cake. Donna is too busy talking and laughing with the other girls to notice when I leave the VIP booth with Kasim.

We're out of the club and in Dray's car. Again, I'm in Donna's seat, on the passenger side.

"Where are you taking me?" I ask Kasim when I notice that he's driving toward the tall buildings downtown. We're on Livernois, and before long, after a few turns, we're on Atwater Street pulling into a parking lot. I can see the dark stretch of water greeting me in the distance. I smile because rivers are Ezili's home. Kasim comes around to open the door for me, and he places his coat over my shoulders.

The air is cold and sharp. There are tall and wide buildings on one side of the street and trees, walkways, and the river on the other side. It's as if they were building this city until it reached the very edge of the river here. I pull up the hood of the coat and pull down the sleeves over my bare hands. When we reach the brightly lit walkway near the river, Kasim's phone rings and he answers it.

"Yo, man, I just had to take Fab home right quick. I'll be back soon—just save a bottle for me. . . . What?" He takes the phone away from his ear. "Fab, Dray wants to talk to you."

My stomach twists. I start to shake my head, but I change my mind. I take his phone. "Hello?"

"Why you gotta bounce like that, Fab? Your cousin's looking all over the place for you. I invited you to celebrate my birthday with me. I dropped some coins just so you look good for my boy. And you just gonna leave without saying shit?"

"I didn't feel well." I glance at Kasim, who is holding his head down with both hands in his pockets. "Tell Donna I'm sorry."

"Oh, tell *Donna* you're sorry? Even though it was my party? Okay."

I don't say anything and Kasim sees my face, so he takes the phone from me.

"Yo, Dray, I'll check you in a few, a'ight? Happy birthday, man." Kasim inhales long and deep and puts the phone in his pocket. "Dray just looks out for me, that's all. Don't matter if it's dudes or girls—he just has my back."

I turn to head back to the car. "Take me home."

"No. Not yet," he says, and grabs both my hands and pulls me in. "Can we just chill for a minute?"

I lean into him. He eases his arms around my waist and my whole body warms. I rest my head on his shoulder. But he steps back and takes my face and kisses my forehead, then kisses me long and deep.

I am two sides of the same coin. Ezili has made all of me like honey—sweet, sticky, and oozing under Kasim's hold. But Ezili-Danto has lit a fire inside of me—with rage in my heart and a dagger in my hand, I want nothing more than to slice away this sore named Dray so I can free Donna and get my mother back.

NINETEEN

"**WHY YOU NOT** answering my calls?" Dray yells from down-stairs. His anger seems to make the whole house shake.

Donna has locked herself in her bedroom. She called Dray this morning and cursed him out after someone told her that the police caught him hooking up with another girl. I was there that night when Donna got the text from a friend, and then a phone call, and then Pri and Chantal couldn't stop talking about it, telling her to break it off with him for good.

Matant Jo is trying to make him leave, but he keeps calling Donna's name. "Ma, Ma," Dray says. "I just want to talk, that's all."

I don't hear Matant Jo respond to him.

"Yo, D. I swear, I'm about to come up there and get you," Dray says.

Then Pri bursts out of the room and yells down, "No, you better the fuck not come up here, or I got something for that ass, Dray!"

Chantal is not home now to talk some sense into the situation. I text her, but she doesn't answer.

"Where's Donna? Just tell her to give me a second. That's all. Baby? I'm sorry. I love you." Dray tries to make his voice sound sad.

"Oh, hell no!" Pri says. "Donna, go deal with that nigga before I run down there and drop-kick him in his balls."

"Donna?" Matant Jo shouts from downstairs. "Come talk to him. All these years of him running after you, and you running after him, it's now you want to hide? Come down here. Curse him out. Tell him how you feel. But I swear on your father's grave, if he puts a hand on you, it will be his last time."

A chill runs down my spine when I hear my aunt say this. It's as if she's slowly coming back to life. I get a hint of the Jo who everyone respects around here. I get up from Chantal's bed and open the door a little to see more of what's going on.

Donna bursts out of her room and only stands at the top of the stairs. "A white girl, Dray? You got busted while you were with a motherfuckin' white girl?"

"That's why you don't gotta worry about her!" Dray yells back.

"Fuck you! Get the fuck outta my house!"

"Final-fuckin'-ly," Pri says. "It took a white girl for her to finally see him for the piece of shit that he is."

"Donna!" Dray calls out. And then footsteps up the stairs.

I quickly hide behind Chantal's door. I don't want Dray to even know that I'm here.

"Dray, I done told you not to come up here," Pri says. Through the cracked door, I can see that her socked feet are really close to Dray's boots. Donna has stepped back and is quiet.

"Hey, hey, hey!" Matant Jo calls from downstairs. "Dray, you know better!"

"Jo, I'm just trying to talk to Donna, that's all. Baby? Come on. I swear, you ain't got to worry about nothing."

"Tell me something, Dray." Donna's bare feet step closer to Dray's boots. "Did Q have to bail out your white girl, too? Is she moving weight for you, or you just have her around to suck your dick every once in a while?"

"How you even know about this shit? You a fuckin' snitch, D?"

I'm trying to figure everything out as the words swim in my head. *Q. Bail out. Snitch.* Something happened and didn't happen at the same time. Dray got arrested and maybe it was because of the information I sent to the detective. But he's here

190

now. He's out of jail. Something went wrong. My information was no good.

Dray steps closer to Donna, but Pri blocks him, and Matant Jo is now in the frame. I can tell that one of her slippered feet holds up most of her weight, but I've never seen her have the energy to come up the stairs before. I close my eyes and hope that no one calls my name.

"Get out! Get the fuck out, Drayton!" Matant Jo's voice explodes.

"I'm not trying to start no shit, Jo. I just want Donna to listen to me!"

"Out of my house!"

Dray's footsteps head back down the stairs.

Then he says, "Donna. I love you. I swear to God, I love you!"

"Shut the fuck up!" Pri yells back, but Dray is already out the door.

I rush to the window to make sure that he leaves, that he is finally out of Donna's life. But before he gets back into his car, he looks up toward the window and sees me. For a moment, our eyes meet. I stare back at him, hard, squinting. If only he could hear my thoughts saying, *I will destroy you,* malfekté. He is the first to look away.

He might be Baron Samedi, guardian of the cemetery, but he is digging his own grave, and all I have to do is push him in.

TWENTY

I MISS RICE and beans. I miss spicy stewed chicken and red snapper seasoned to the bone. I miss *banan peze*, fried plantains—not like the too-sweet ones that Chantal gets from a Jamaican restaurant. I miss the hot sun and sweating all day and the beach and eating cold *fresco* with my friends and long walks up and down hills and Cola Lakay and deep-fried beef patties. I miss my mother.

I can tell that I'm skinnier because the thin gold bracelet I've been wearing since I turned sixteen now slips down my hand. I have to keep pushing it up to my wrist. Nothing tastes good. The most exercise I get is the short steps in front of the house and the stairs at school. Nothing else. Still, I'm skinny and it's not a pretty kind of skinny like fashion models. It's my body slowly giving up on everything, including the flesh on my bones.

But I know this won't last. I just need one more piece of information on Dray that I can give to Detective Stevens. This is the drought before the cleansing rain, as my mother would say—the storm cloud before the sun.

"You on a diet or something?" Imani asks. She's sitting next to me in the loud cafeteria. I've managed to block out all the noise to let my thoughts wander. I don't notice how I'm picking at the ham, lettuce, and tomatoes from the sandwich and pushing aside the thick bread and slices of cheese.

"Come with me to the supermarket later," I say. "I can cook you a good meal. Come over."

"This is like the tenth time you asked me, Fab. Ain't no way in hell I'm going to, one, the Three Bees' house, and two, the west side."

"Donna stopped bothering you, right?"

"Yeah, that don't mean shit. I could just be walking to class one day, minding my own business, and her twin might decide that she remembers why she had beef with me in the first place." She takes a big bite from her sandwich.

"I got your back, Imani," I say.

She coughs and almost chokes. "What'd you say?"

"I got your back."

She laughs and has to spit out her chewed-up food. "Say it again."

I don't because I've heard that before. A laugh followed by "say it again" means that I've said something that makes me sound stupid.

"Daesia!" Imani calls out to her friend who's coming to sit next to us. "Fab said she got my back."

"Oh, you the Fourth Bee, now?" Daesia asks.

I shake my head.

"Who's the Fourth Bee?" another girl asks, and sits right next to me. Her name is Tammie.

Imani points to me with her chin while still laughing.

"No, I am not," I say, taking a bite of the too-salty ham.

"But we good, though, 'cause she says she has my back," Imani says. I can't tell if she's serious or making fun of me.

"If you got her back, then you gotta have our back, too," Daesia says. "We've been friends with her for much longer than you."

"I'm not a Fourth Bee," I say really loud, so everyone who might be listening can hear me.

"If she says she's not the Fourth Bee, then she's not," Imani says, and smiles at me.

"Good, 'cause I wouldn't want to be around you if you were," Daesia says. "Why do they have to be so nasty to everybody?"

"'Cause people were nasty to them," I say.

"Not us," Tammie says.

"'Cause they don't even see us unless somebody's man does," Imani adds.

"That's not true," I say.

"Donna didn't even know my name until she saw me on Instagram sitting on Dray's lap."

"Is that why you started hanging with me?" I ask.

Imani laughs again. "No. You just looked lost, that's all. And you have to say the *h* sound when you say 'hanging,' okay?"

So I say, "Hanging."

Imani makes a breathing sound from the back of her throat and I try to do the same. Now Daesia and Tammie are laughing.

"It's a lost cause," Tammie says. "Why don't you teach us some Haitian curse words instead?"

I smile, because not even my own cousins have asked me to do that. So I start with *bouzin*. Then I move on to *kolan guete*, and *zozo*, *bounda*, *coco*. All the words that would make my mother rip my lips from my face if she heard me right now. Watching my friends try to twist their mouths to say these words, I laugh as much as my cousins do when I try to say American curse words. I laugh so hard that my belly hurts; tears come out of my eyes.

Until someone slices through all our laughter with a stupid question: "Is your name Fabulous? You Pri and them's cousin?"

I don't answer, because at this point, everyone knows who I am. I don't even turn to see who this girl is.

"Excuse me, I asked you a question. Do you go by *Fabulous*?"

I turn to see a regular girl, not tall, not short, not fat or skinny. Just regular. Except for the way she asks me the question, as if it's an accusation.

"Yes, and you are?" I ask.

"Tonesha. Your cousins know me. You messing with Kasim?"

"Oh, lord. Here we go," Imani says. I know this feeling. These questions and warnings are an attack. It doesn't matter if it's in English or Creole. In Port-au-Prince or Detroit—a *bouzin* will always be a *bouzin*. And I remember my cousin's words: *If these girls think you're scared and that you're not gonna fight back, they will mess with you.*

"Yes, he's my boyfriend" is all I say.

"Not for long, bitch. My cousin Raquel already claimed Kasim." Tonesha starts to walk away.

A fire burns in my belly. No girl, no matter how tough and mean she is, is going to scare me away from Kasim. He is mine and I am his. "Tell your cousin to stay away from my boyfriend!" I yell.

"What?" The girl turns around just as the whole cafeteria lets out a series of *Ooooooh*s.

I don't give her the satisfaction of repeating myself.

Tonesha looks around at everyone in the cafeteria, as if making sure that her audience is in place. She steps closer to me. I don't move.

"Yo, I don't care if you're from Haiti or motherfucking Iraq," she says, pointing her finger in my face. "You need to back up off Kasim. And that shit is a warning."

Another series of *Ooooohs*!

Someone calls her name and tells her to leave me alone. But she doesn't.

"Get away from me, bitch," I say, staring right into her eyes.

Imani grabs my shoulder, but I tighten my body. I won't be the first one to back down. I am like a rock now.

"Tonesha, Pri's coming!" another person shouts.

"Ay yo, Fab! You all right?" Pri calls out from some other end of the cafeteria.

"Yeah, she's a'ight!" Tonesha shouts back.

"I wasn't talking to you!" Pri says.

But before she can step between me and Tonesha, the bell rings and teachers start to make their way to the crowd of kids surrounding us. I relax now, and Pri comes to pull me away.

"Don't let no bitch get to you," she whispers into my ear as we leave the cafeteria. "But the next time she tries to pull that shit, I'ma smack that *bouzin* one time so she won't step to you like that ever again."

I laugh because my cousin said something in Creole. I laugh the same way she has laughed at me.

That afternoon, Kasim has his old, ugly car back and it feels like the first day we went out together. I didn't know he was coming to pick me up after school, so I still have on that ugly weave from Unique Hair Essentials. My lips are chapped and I dig for crust in the corners of my eyes before I get into his car. I want him to wait a little bit in front of the school so Tonesha can see me with him and she can run and tell her cousin.

I glide on some lip gloss before he leans over to kiss me.

"Why you go and do that for?" he asks.

"Because my lips were no good," I say.

"I want your lips naked, like I want your—" He stops.

"What? Say it. My body?"

"You said it, not me." He laughs.

I let him kiss me right in front of the school. Then someone bangs on the hood of the car.

"Get a room!" It's Pri. "No, no, no. I take that back. Keep your hands to yourself, young man." She points to Kasim and they both laugh.

I watch as Pri and Donna walk down the block. I don't know where they are going, but I'm glad that they've been leaving me alone. I thought they would be babysitting me this whole time, but they have their own lives, and I have mine, thank goodness.

Then I spot that girl named Tonesha walking past the car. "You know her?" I ask.

"Who? Tonesha? Why? She messing with you?"

"She came to my face today."

He starts the car. It's noisier now, as if whatever he fixed has gotten worse. "She *came* to your face? You mean, she was all up in your face?"

"I had to protect you, Kasim," I say with a smile.

He looks at me as he drives down Vernor Highway, and I don't even ask where he's taking me because I'm so glad to be spending time with him. A grin spreads across his face and my insides go warm.

"Damn. Sounds like you held your own, shorty—tellin' Tonesha 'he's my man.' In fact, you should tell your whole school, the whole west side, east side, all of Detroit that I'm your man."

"No, *you* tell Detroit that I'm your girl," I say.

"A'ight," he says. He rolls down his window and sticks his head out a little bit. "Ay yo, Detroit! This girl right here, Fabulous, she's the one! Feel me, Detroit! Fabulous . . ."

"Kasim!" I yell, and try to pull him back in by the sleeve of his coat. "Keep your eyes on the road!" I almost want him to keep yelling it out just so Tonesha and this cousin of hers can hear it.

He laughs. "Wait. I don't even know your last name and I'm in love with you. You got the same last name as your cousins, right? Fabulous François?"

I laugh while still clutching his sleeve. "My name is not even Fabulous. It's Fabiola. Fabiola Toussaint!" I say, but it's the words *I'm in love with you* that linger in my mind. I want him to say it again—to repeat it over and over so that I'm sure I heard him correctly the first time.

"Yeah, but I like Fabulous François better. It sounds important and shit. Like you're some movie star."

"No. My name is my name and you can't change it. What about you? Are you Broke Carter? You have Dray's last name?"

"Oh, how you gonna know Dray's last name before you know mine? Huh, Fabulous?"

I don't answer, because I've only heard Dray's last name once and it was from the detective. I slipped. I wasn't supposed to let him know that. "I heard Donna say it," I lie.

"Well, no. It's not Carter. It's Anderson."

"Broke Anderson. I like Broke Carter instead. Like this broke car."

He laughs hard and for a long time and I'm afraid that he's not watching the road. I laugh, too, but I keep my eyes on Livernois Avenue for him.

Finally, he stops laughing and breathes out, "Damn."

"What happened?" I ask.

"You got me," he says.

"I got you what?" I ask.

While still holding the steering wheel and keeping his eyes on the road, he takes his free hand and cups it over his chest. He motions as if he's grabbing something and then gives it over to me. "Here," he says. "It's yours."

Slowly, I take his invisible heart and hold it close to mine. I hug it. I know he sees me do that out of the corner of his eye.

Then he rests his hand on my lap, opening up his palm for me to take. We hold hands until he has to make a left turn down Joy Road.

At home, I have homework, and dinner to make, and dishes to wash. But I could spend the rest of the afternoon, and evening, and night sitting in this car with Kasim.

"I gotta go work the evening shift," he says as he parks on American Street and turns off the engine. "But you could come do your homework at the café."

"No," I almost whisper. "Can we save a little bit of this for tomorrow, and the next day, and the next day after that?"

"A'ight," he whispers, and leans over to kiss me.

Then I take his hand, the one that gave me his heart, and kiss it.

I don't let him get out to open the door for me. But he grabs the back of my skirt as I'm getting out of the car. I gently tug it away. He's smiling big and I almost don't want to close the door on him.

"Tomorrow," I say.

I spot Papa Legba on his bucket, smoking his cigar. I think he tips his hat at me. But I'm not sure. Maybe this is Papa Legba's way of saying this is good. This is very good.

TWENTY-ONE

SOMEONE IS POUNDING on the front door. It eases into my dreams at first. Chantal steps over my body on the air mattress to get to the door and I'm pulled out of sleep completely. My cousins are whispering to one another at the top of the steps. No one turns on any lights. There's more banging on the door and I go over to the window to look outside.

"Fab, get away from that window!" Chantal whisper-yells. "Stay in here and mind your business!"

I duck down and let the curtain fall closed, but still I listen, confused.

"Why the fuck would he bring those two goons with him?" Pri says. "The one time Ma goes out is when this nigga decides to show up. Punk ass."

"Shut up!" Chantal says.

I listen as my cousins open the door. I thought it would be Dray, but it's not his voice that yells, "What the fuck y'all got me waiting out here for all this time?"

I don't listen to Chantal. I tiptoe to the top of the stairs, lying down on the floor to make sure I'm invisible. The single streetlight from the corner shines on the three men in the doorway. I don't recognize any of them—two tall and wide, and the one in the middle is thin and old, older than Matant Jo.

"We didn't know it was you," Pri lies.

The older man chuckles. "After you done looked out the window and saw my car, you didn't know it was me? Get outta here with that bullshit, *Pri*."

All three of my cousins back up into the living room as the three men step into the house. They shut the door and someone turns on the lights. I inch back away from the stairs and hope that no one calls me down.

"I've been trying to get in contact with you for weeks now. You been ignoring my calls. Same thing you're doing to Dray, Donna," the man says.

He sounds calm and smart, like a teacher. He's wearing a nice long black coat, and I can see dress pants and shiny shoes peeking out from underneath it. The other two men are not dressed up, so they look like bodyguards.

"Q, we just been lying low these past couple of months.

That's all. The news, the cops, all that shit got us hiding out," Pri says.

Chantal tugs Pri's arm. Then she says, "We just don't want anything coming back to us or to you, Uncle Q."

I'm not sure if I hear correctly, so I turn my ear downstairs.

I search my memory for this Uncle Q's story—his name has come up several times before but I've never met him, never seen him, until now. From Kasim's story: Uncle Q bought the tickets to that dance show; Uncle is like a father to him; my uncle Phillip took a bullet for this Q. And from Dray's story: he owns the club with the purple door where there's a gun and dogs and secrets; Uncle Q threw a party for my aunt's fortieth birthday. Q is a drug dealer. Q is Dray's uncle.

"I'm here to collect, ladies. It's payday. It's a damn shame I gotta come all the way out here," Q says, as cool as rainwater.

"We need more time, Uncle Q. We had to toss all of it. We're not trying to sell some messed-up batch," Chantal says.

I hold my head up. The wood floor beneath the carpet squeaks under my weight. I freeze. My eyes burn because they're open so wide. I don't blink. My heart races and the air around me is not enough, so I breathe slowly, trying to calm down because that older man is Q, and my cousins need more time, and they were supposed to sell something. But what? What?

"Not my fucking problem. Twenty Gs," Q says.

"Wait a minute," Chantal says. "We only got fifteen worth. Where'd that extra five come from?"

"Interest. Insurance. To cover my ass for whatever the fuck y'all just did over there in the Pointe to get that white girl killed."

The words swim in my head. *White girl killed. My cousins. My cousins got that white girl killed.*

"Q, for real?" Pri asks. "That's not on us. You sold us bad shit."

Q reaches into his coat pocket. My cousins shift a little, and he pulls out something that he puts into his mouth—a toothpick. "None of my business how those kids choose to use my products. Everything was fine by the time it got to you."

"That's not how it works, Q," Chantal says as calm as ice. "If word gets around that some girl died from shit she got from us, no more business. That's the end of our deal."

I sit up. The floor squeaks again, but I don't care. *Some girl died from shit she got from us* echoes in my ears loud and clear, as if it's the voice of God. *Some girl died from shit she got from us. . . .* Those words pour down on me like sharp, heavy raindrops. No. Stones. They beat against my head, so I stand to my feet. *Some girl died from shit she got from us*, I repeat to myself.

The words are so heavy that they make everything sink inside me.

My cousins. My cousins sold drugs. My cousins sold the drugs that killed the white girl. Madison. The girl whose death Detective Stevens is investigating.

I realize the detective is wrong. Dray was not the one who

sold the drugs. I can't just let Dray go to jail for something he didn't do. My cousins. My cousins are the ones who are responsible. But do I tell that to the detective? No! No way. My cousins will go to jail. And my mother is already in something like jail.

My head spins. There are questions and questions that whirl around my mind like a tornado, and they slowly make their way up to my throat to form one deep, angry wail. I hold on to the banister. I don't know if I'm going to just fall over, or throw up on everybody downstairs. The floor squeaks again, but they are still talking. I brace myself because I have to hear more. I have to hear the hows and whys and what-ifs.

"Chantal, honey. You're the smart one." Uncle Q steps closer to her. "You're acting like you don't know how to count money. Your mother didn't teach you anything?"

"Leave our mother outta this, Q," she says. "She never pushed for you."

"Your mother did all she could to keep y'all off the streets, but y'all still wanna play with the big boys. 'Specially you, Pri. You just looking for trouble, ain't you? I need twenty by the end of the month. Don't fuck with my money, *Three Bees.*" He steps over to Pri and taps two fingers on her temple.

Pri pushes his hand away.

He laughs. "Fiery little bitch, ain't you? Just like your daddy."

Chantal quickly pulls Pri back before she can do anything.

She then grabs Donna's arm and they all step away from Q and his bodyguards.

The men leave. But my cousins don't move until they're sure that Q's car has turned the corner and driven several blocks out of the neighborhood. And I'm as still as a rock, even as my cousins sit on the couch. They're quiet for much too long. Finally, they begin to speak again.

"How much you think Ma got?" Donna speaks for the first time since the men left.

"Yo, you shittin' me right now, D?" Pri hisses.

"What if—" Donna starts to say.

"Nope," Chantal cuts her off. "Don't even try it. I already know what you're gonna say."

"What am I gonna say?"

"Don't you even think about bringing Dray into this," Chantal says.

I sneak partway down the stairs and peek under the banister.

"All this time, did I ever say anything to him? Not once did he even guess what was going on," Donna says.

Pri starts clapping really slowly, then really fast. She gets up and claps in Donna's face. "Bra-the-fuck-vo! You didn't sell out your sisters to your man. You deserve a fucking cookie!"

Donna pushes her hands away. Pri shoves Donna's head.

"Would y'all stop! And be quiet!" Chantal points to the ceiling and I know it's because of me.

I ease back up the stairs again. But before I can even rush back into the bedroom, Pri has already leaped up to find me near the banister. Chantal and Donna are right behind her.

"How long you been there, Fab?" Pri asks.

I stand up. I don't take my eyes away from Pri and I don't answer her question.

"Handle that, Chant. That's your girl," she says.

"No," Chantal says. "We're handling this together."

"Yes," I say. "Please do. I have a lot of questions."

"Aw, shit," Pri says. "Here's my answer so we can all get back to bed: none of your business!"

"You sell drugs?" I yell. It wasn't supposed to be that loud, but it just bursts out as if I'm a bottle of Pepsi that my cousins shook really hard and then opened the top, and I yell out again, "You sell drugs?"

"Shut up, Fabiola!" Pri yells in my face. "Shut the fuck up! Chantal, handle that."

"Don't tell me to shut up!" I yell back. This time, I'm in Pri's face. "I live here, too. This is my house, too. You tell me if you are selling drugs. You tell me everything!"

Chantal pulls me away from her. Pri has her head down and is shaking it over and over again.

"What, what, what?" I yell at her again. "You want to fight me, Pri? I will fight you if you don't tell me the truth."

"Yo." She laughs. "Chantal, please calm her the fuck down."

Chantal grabs both my arms and pushes me against the

bathroom door. "Fabiola. Calm down. There's no reason for you to be getting all hyped for something that has nothing to do with you."

I inhale and exhale. This has everything to do with me, but they don't know it. Everything has changed and I will not be able to get my mother back. I cannot give Detective Stevens my cousins. I cannot get my manman home.

Pri paces back and forth in the short, narrow hallway. Donna covers her face with her hands, and I can't tell if she's crying or not.

"The girl on the news?" I ask, a little bit calmer now. "The one the people are protesting for? Is that your fault? Did you do that?"

Chantal lets go of me. "Now why in the world would you connect a dead white girl to us, huh? Why would you even think we have anything to do with that?"

"I'm not stupid," I say. For a moment, I am afraid I've said too much. Detective Stevens has told me too much. "I heard that man, Uncle Q , say it. Grosse Pointe Park, right?"

They're all quiet. Then Donna starts to walk into her bedroom.

"No! You have to tell me what's going on. There is all this money. I don't even see Matant Jo working. Is that what you have been sending to Haiti all this time? Drug money? If everything I ever had in my life is because of drug money, I need to know." I speak as if my words are running. I'm out of breath. My heart is a conga drum. I wipe sweat from my forehead.

"It wasn't always drug money," Chantal says.

"Chant!" Pri calls out. "What you doing?"

"She's family. She asked a question, so I'm telling her."

Pri rushes to me and puts her finger in my face. "Fabiola, I swear on my father's grave, if you so much as utter a word to any one of your so-called friends, I will . . . Ooooh! You don't even wanna know." She steps away from me.

Chantal takes my hand and walks me into her bedroom. She sits me down. Donna and Pri come in, turn on a nearby lamp, and close the door behind them. Chantal doesn't let go of my hand. She takes the other one and looks me in the eye. I look her in the eye, too.

"Maybe it was supposed to be Four Bees all along," she says.

Pri sighs long and deep, and she plops down on my mattress. It makes a hissing sound as if the air is slowly escaping.

"Maybe we're not supposed to be like a pyramid," Chantal continues. "'Cause that'll mean somebody would have to be on top. And we don't want nobody falling off."

"Chantal, what the fuck you talkin' about?" Pri asks.

Chantal shushes her. "Maybe you're here to make us more like a square—four points—a solid foundation."

"I can't believe she's turning this shit into a geometry class," Pri mumbles.

I pull my hands away from Chantal. "Don't treat me like a

baby," I say. "How are you going to get the money for that man by the end of the month?"

"I don't know yet. Uncle Q was like a father to us," Donna says. She's standing by the closed door with her arms folded across her chest. A silky scarf is tied around her head and for the first time, I get a good look at her face without all the makeup. I see my face in hers, my mother's face in hers—so small, simple, and pretty. "He looked out for us after our father died."

"Yo, son." Pri sits up on the air mattress now and pounds her fist into her palm with each word she speaks. "He's out fifteen Gs. You think he's gonna let that shit slide?"

"He's not gonna let it slide," Chantal says.

"Wait, wait, wait," I say. "What happened to his money? Why don't you just give it back to him?"

Chantal sighs. "Fabiola, our father was making a drop for Q when he got shot in the back of his head. He wasn't dealing or nothing. He just needed some extra cash, like everybody else around here."

"What?" I breathe. I sit down. I brace myself.

"It wasn't random," she continues. "Our father dipped his toe into the game for just a hot minute. One drop. That's all. So, of course, Q had to pay up for that deal gone bad. So Q gave Ma thirty Gs 'cause we were just little kids and she was struggling really hard to raise us. She didn't know English, and she didn't have any skills. But that money wasn't lasting 'cause Ma was giving it away—a couple hundred here, a couple thousand there, until Q put an end to that. He was like, Yo, they gotta pay you back. So she started loaning out money—a loan shark. And she had to get muscle to back her up because people weren't paying her back at first. So Q hooked her up with some of his boys. And with that kinda weight, she had to have the mouth to back everything else up, too. If her boys couldn't handle business, Ma would just roll up to somebody's house, curse the shit out of them in Creole, and jack them up for all they got. You know why, Fabiola?"

"No. Why?"

"Because of you and your mom," Chantal says. "Catholic school for all three of us out here was just pennies. But your ass over there in Haiti cost her like twenty Gs every year. Your school, money for your mom, your clothes. Hell, all this time, Ma thought y'all were building a mansion near the beach and she swore she'd go back down there to retire.

"But she's getting sick. We don't want her to do this loan-sharking shit anymore. Money was running out. We still gotta live, Fab. We still gotta breathe. Money's just room to breathe, that's all."

I don't even realize when the tears start rolling down my cheeks. I let them fall. I let them drip from my chin, and onto my mother's nightgown, and onto Chantal's blanket. The room is quiet. "What now?" I finally ask.

"What now is that you keep your mouth shut and let us

handle this," Pri says. "As a matter of fact, forget everything you heard and saw tonight. Don't let Ma even read that shit off your forehead."

Chantal nods. "Focus on graduating, Fabiola. That's all."

"My mother," I whisper.

Chantal sighs. "We'll figure something out. I promise."

I don't believe her, because this thing with Uncle Q is a much heavier burden than this aunt they hardly know. They are the ones who are responsible for that girl's death. Not Dray. My cousins. I am at a crossroads again.

Hours pass and my cousins are asleep. I breathe in and pretend that I'm taking in my mother's scent—baby powder and cheap perfume. I hug myself and pretend it's her arms around me, pulling me in close, and kissing me on the forehead, and asking me if I washed my face, if I did my homework, if I made a good, hearty meal for her to eat.

Something pulls me out of bed, out of Chantal's room, out of the house, and onto American Street and Joy Road. Bad Leg is nowhere. His overturned plastic bucket is gone, and the streetlight shines on only the empty lot and me. I am lost. There is no road for me to take. Nothing will lead me to my mother, or clear the way for her to get to me.

I turn to each of the corners—the four directions—as if to bow to every single possibility around me: north, south, east, west. A light rain starts to fall and I think of my cousins. If the old man at the corner called Bad Leg is Papa Legba in the flesh, if Dray with his eye patch and gold cross is Baron Samedi, if Donna with her makeup and pretty things is Ezili and, with her scars, Ezili-Danto, then Chantal and Pri can be my spirit guides, too, as Ogu, the warrior, and one-half of *Les Marassa Jumeaux*, the divine twins who stand for truth, balance, and justice. Maybe even Kasim represents a *lwa* if I look hard enough. They are all here to help.

I run back to the house and reach the door, turn the knob, but it doesn't budge. I twist the knob from right to left, from left to right. It's locked. I almost knock, but something about this door . . . I step back away from it and go down the short front steps. Something about those steps . . . I back away from the house and stand on the narrow patch of brown grass. Something about this house . . . 8800 American Street.

I used to stare at that address whenever those white envelopes with the blue-and-red-striped edges would make their way to our little house in Port-au-Prince. I'd copy the address over and over again, 8800 American Street, because this house was my very first home. But for three short months only. This house is where I became American. This house is the one my mother and I prayed for every night, every morning, and during every ceremony: 8800 American Street.

But maybe, again, my eyes are betraying me, because this house that stands here at the corner, with its doorway almost like a smile, with its windows almost like eyes making fun of everything it sees, seems different.

I walk around the side, to Joy Road, thinking there must be another door I've never seen. Nothing. There's a small backyard protected by a tall gate. No entrance there, either.

I come back around to the front and knock on the door really loud. Finally, I hear heavy footsteps. I guess I didn't hear Matant Jo come in after all. She opens the door, but instead of my aunt's face, or any one of my cousins greeting me, it's an older white man.

I quickly apologize and step back away from the door and run down the steps, thinking that I got turned around somehow. But I look back at the house, now with its door closed. It's still 8800 American Street. So I go back and knock again. Now it's a white woman who opens the door. I apologize. She closes the door. I don't move because the number on the house still reads 8800. So I knock again. This time, a younger white man opens the door.

"Excuse me," I ask. "Is this eighty-eight hundred?"

I must've scared him, because his eyes open wide, wide, and he shuts the door. But before I knock again, he's back. This time I'm staring at a gun. A gun!

And the only thing I can do is throw my hands up to my face and scream.

It goes off with a loud bang.

I scream and scream until I hear my name.

"Fabiola! Fabiola!"

I open my eyes to bright light and Chantal's face standing over me, calling my name over and over again until I stop screaming and realize that I've been in bed all along.

"Are you okay?" Chantal asks.

"No," I say. As my heart calms down, as my breath softens, I get up to work on my altar.

I tie my head with my mother's white scarf, fill the white enamel mug with water from the bathroom sink, light another tea candle with a match, and recite my prayer to Papa Legba once again.

THE STORY OF 8800
AMERICAN STREET

There was work here in Detroit—cars, houses, factories, highways. Here was the American dream built brick by brick, screw by screw, concrete over dirt.

So Adrian Weiss and his wife, Ruth, moved into 8800 American Street in July 1924, after that long journey from Poland, and Ellis Island, and the tenements of New York City. He'd been working in the Ford River Rouge complex for the last five years when Ruth gave birth to their first child in the middle of a snowstorm. Adrian came home two days later, drunk, smelly, bruised, and without a job because Henry Ford had zero tolerance for drunkards and their bathtub gin. So why not gin? Adrian loved it just as much as he loved the Model T. And there was more money with the Purple Gang and its bootlegging.

Months later, Ruth hid money beneath the mattresses, in Mason jars, in the ice box, in the backyard. Adrian liked to flaunt his money, even during the Great Depression of 1929, when the other husbands were let go from their jobs, and the women knocked on the door of 8800 American Street for some bread and milk or for some of that well-hidden money.

So maybe it was the jealous husbands on American Street, or unpaid debt owed to some members of the Purple Gang, that led to the shooting of Adrian Weiss on the corner of American Street and Joy Road. And maybe it was because of this first act of violence at the crossroads of hopes and dreams that death lingered around that house like a baby ghost.

So in 1942, Ohio native and father of one Wilson Coolidge, who'd bought the house from Ruth Weiss four years earlier, was struck by a car on the corner of American and Joy.

Father of two, Alabama native, and son of a sharecropper, Lester Charles Walker was one of American Street's very first black residents in 1947. He was shot and killed by his white neighbor just as he stepped out of 8800.

The old families, whose grandfathers and fathers worked at the Ford plant, were fleeing the neighborhood as if it was the second coming of the black plague. White flight, they called it. And it swept over most of Detroit like a giant bird of prey.

It was no use selling 8800 since kinfolk from Alabama, Georgia, and South Carolina were now moving in, and on most days, they gathered on the sidewalks and the porches for gossip and cookouts.

Death had moved away from 8800 American Street and traveled to the many broken parts of the city. So during the 12th Street riot in July 1967, Lester Junior was struck by a single bullet to the head.

The youngest Walker son rented out 8800 all through the eighties and nineties when Death claimed the lives of dealers and junkies alike. Until the day came when a black man in a suit and with a funny accent decided to call it his little dream house. He wanted what the very first residents wanted: to be American and to have some Joy.

So in 2000, Jean-Phillip François, the Haitian immigrant and the first occupant to actually land a job at a car factory—the Chrysler plant—paid the city three thousand dollars in cash for that little house on American Street.

And maybe because the little house had been revived with the sounds of babies and the scent of warm meals and love and hopes and dreams, Death woke from its long sleep to claim the life of Haitian immigrant and father of three Jean-Phillip François with a single bullet to the head outside the Chrysler plant.

Death parked itself on that corner of American and Joy, some days as still as stone, other days singing cautionary songs and delivering telltale riddles, waiting for the day when one girl would ask to open the gates to the other side.

TWENTY-TWO

MY SCALP ITCHES, but I can't get to it because of this stupid weave. The fake hair is sewn to my own braided hair and my scalp doesn't have room to breathe. And it was all for nothing. I turned myself into someone else just so I could get information on Dray, but he was the wrong one.

He comes around less now, and I hang out with Pri and Donna more. Or maybe they are keeping me close. Only a few days have passed since the thing with Q and me finding out what my cousins really do for money.

But it doesn't change who they are—Chantal still sticks to her books and is worried about paying for her classes next semester. She shows me how to fill out financial aid and scholarship forms. "You're a citizen, so you'll be good. But make sure you take advantage of every penny, you hear me?" she says.

I don't trust it because my mother filled out American forms that promised her things, too.

Pri still likes a girl from afar. I hear her singing in the shower one night—a love song. She sings Taj's name. Her voice is smooth and it reaches me all the way on my mattress. It sounds like it's filled with the shards of her broken heart. So when she comes out, I ask her, "How will you ever know if Taj feels the same?"

"I won't. And I'm okay with that," Pri says. "That's what gives me my edge. Probably gonna walk around with a little chip on my shoulder all my life."

"But you deserve every good thing," I tell her.

"And the bad things?" she asks.

I don't have an answer for her.

I borrow more of Donna's clothes now. This is how we've become closer. I give in to all the things I've always liked: jeans that show off my curves, light makeup—not too much, just lip gloss and mascara—and beautiful hairstyles that highlight my eyes and cheekbones as Donna says. My mother is not here to judge me. So I experiment with different looks.

And Kasim. Kasim. I have been ignoring him since the night I found out.

My cousins make sure that I come with them whenever they go out together. I'm never in the house alone with Matant

Jo. One day, we drove somewhere to pay a bill. Another day, we went grocery shopping. This morning, we're going out to eat chicken and waffles, a dish I've never had.

Before we leave, I hear Matant Jo calling Chantal's name from her bedroom. She comes out and she's all dressed up in a nice sweater and a wig. She's been making herself look nice and going out. She's not worried about her sister anymore, it seems. But I am. She reminds me of my mother when she's like this—all smiles and sunny days. But Chantal tells me not to get used to it.

"Where y'all going?" she asks. "Is there room for me?"

"Hell yeah!" Pri says.

And soon, I'm in the backseat, squeezed between the twins while Chantal drives and Aunt Jo sits in the passenger seat. My heart swells because this is starting to feel like a family. My heart deflates because my mother is starting to feel farther and farther away. I shake the thought from my mind, because thinking of my mother forces me to think of my cousins and their drugs, which makes me think of Detective Stevens, and Dray, and Kasim. Kasim. My heart swells again.

We drive down Livernois Avenue to a place called Kuzzo's Chicken and Waffles.

"This is your spot, *cuzz*," Pri jokes, and rubs the top of my head.

When Chantal parks the car, I notice her looking every which way, as if making sure nothing is going to jump out of the corners of this neighborhood to attack us. Donna and Pri are looking around, too, and I soon realize that they think Q might be here. This is the only thing I've seen them be afraid of—Q and his threat.

Matant Jo is still all smiles and sunshine and has no idea what's going on with her daughters, or even me, or even her sister. If she finds out about all of this, I wonder if it will break her.

The restaurant is full of people, and this reminds me of my first date with Kasim, when we saw the Alvin Ailey performance. I shake that from my mind, too, because it makes me think of the tickets, which makes me think of Uncle Q, which makes me scared for my cousins.

The whole time at the restaurant, Pri keeps an eye on me, as if I will shout out their secret to their mother at any moment. Even as they joke and eat, I'm quiet and try to enjoy this fried chicken and waffles. Pri forces me to pour syrup over my chicken, too. She's sitting next to me when my phone rings and I recognize Detective Stevens's number. Pri looks at my phone. I don't hide it from her, and I'm glad that I never typed in the detective's name.

"Who's that? Imani?" she asks.

I nod and don't answer the phone.

"You didn't answer it?" Pri says. "So you cuttin' off Kasim *and* Imani? Too much Detroit drama for you, huh?"

"No," I lie. "It's just . . . I want to eat, that's all."

"That's right, Fabiola," Matant Jo says, smiling. "You see,

she has manners. No talking on the phone while you're out for brunch with your family, right, Faboubou!"

"Get outta here with that, Ma!" Pri jokes. "You stay talking on the phone, *and* chewing with your mouth open, *and* cursing at the table. Don't let your aunt fool you, Fab."

Everyone is all smiles. Donna is happy, too, even though she's not with Dray anymore. And Chantal is having small talk with her mother about the weather, the food, and her classes.

I can't finish my meal. The syrup is too sweet and there's more oily skin on the chicken than actual chicken. But my cousins and aunt devour it as if it's their last meal.

My phone rings again. It's Detective Stevens.

"Answer it!" Pri says.

I start to get up from my seat, but Pri grabs the phone from my hand and answers it for me.

"Hello?" she says, and my insides turn to ice. "Hello?"

Then she gives me the phone. Detective Stevens hung up, and I exhale.

"We need to upgrade your phone" is all Pri says.

Aunt Jo pays for the meal with cash. I can't help but stare at the three twenties and one ten, and remember the pile of cash that she gave me. When the waitress comes back with the change, Aunt Jo hands it to me. I shake my head and don't take it.

"Your whole life I've been sending you and your mother money, and it's now you want to reject it?" Matant Jo says.

Pri takes it for me instead. My aunt stares at me as if I've just offended her.

As we're leaving, Kasim walks in with Dray. My heart skips. I don't want to see him. I can't see him. He's not supposed to be here. There is no room for him in my heart right now.

He greets Aunt Jo first, reminding her that they've met a few times already. Dray does the same, but my aunt shoos him away as if he's just a *vagabon*. She stares him in the eye. "You took my baby girl from me since she was twelve. You got into her head and made her think she was in love. She fought me for you. And now you think I'm going to let you win, again?" Matant Jo says.

Donna walks to the car, opens the back door, and gets in without saying a word to Dray.

I want to applaud Matant Jo. Here is where I see a lot of my own mother in her. If Manman was here, she would cut Dray down to a billion pieces if she knew how he treated her niece. And now Matant Jo has come alive.

"Donna, come on!" Dray calls out, ignoring what my aunt has just said. Each time he tries to take a step closer to the car, both Pri and Chantal get in his way.

As I'm watching all this, Kasim takes my hand and asks if he can call me tonight.

"I don't know" is all I say.

He reaches over to kiss me on the cheek, but I stop him.

"I miss you," he says.

"It's too much," I say.

"Too much? What's going on, Fabulous? You know I can see when you're looking at my texts."

"I'm busy."

"Busy? I done seen all your cousins, Imani, your other friends . . . But you just straight up disappeared. Every time I ask for you, they give me some bullshit answer. 'Oh, she's studying, she joined a club, she went home . . .' What's up, Fabulous?" He holds out his hand, but I don't take it.

"Things are complicated now, Kasim," I say. The words are stuck in my throat.

"Complicated? Don't tell me you're going back to Haiti." He keeps trying to take my hand and I keep pulling away.

"No, just . . . I have to help my mom. I like you, Kasim. But I have to focus. . . . Too many things happening now." I cross my arms and look every which way. I don't want to see his face. I can't look into his eyes.

"For real, Fab? What you sayin'?"

"I . . . I can't . . ." I shake my head. I inhale deep because this is all a lie. But I have to do this.

"You can't? We didn't even get started yet. What about saving a little bit for tomorrow, and the next day, and the next day after that?" He keeps trying to look into my eyes. I keep turning my head.

"There's no more left," I say.

"For real, Fab? You serious?"

"Yes." I walk away.

He reaches out and the tips of his fingers brush against my shoulder. I don't look back as I open the car door and slide into the backseat.

Pretending that I don't like him anymore breaks my heart. I don't want to do this to him, but I feel as if I don't have a choice. Before I allow my heart to sink and melt once again, I think of what I must do. My mother is the one who will make my life complete here, not him. I have to sacrifice something in order to get her here. Until then, there is no room for Kasim in my heart.

It's so quiet on the car ride back home that I can hear everyone's breath. Me and Donna have the same rhythm—we both have let go of something heavy and deep.

TWENTY-THREE

TODAY IS THANKSGIVING—a day for families to come together and give thanks, my cousins tell me. I remember how my aunt and cousins used to call us in Haiti to wish us a happy Thanksgiving. We never knew what it meant, so we just replied, "Oh, *mesi*. Same to you!"

Matant Jo has come back to life, and the last few days have been a crazy cyclone of making lists of foods we want to eat, rushing to the supermarket, waiting on long lines, and chopping, and slicing, and seasoning. My cousins are not involved; it's just me and my aunt. Pri has asked for pies—pumpkin and sweet potato. Donna wants something called cranberry sauce. Chantal asks for Haitian rice and beans. At first, Matant Jo seems like she has it all under control. The pots are ready, and the ingredients are out on the table and counters ready to be prepared. She's humming and telling jokes and I'm only here to help.

But now when I walk back into the kitchen, I see her holding her head as if she is about to pass out.

"Matant! Are you okay?" I help her over to a chair and give her a glass of water to drink.

"Fabiola, you have to finish. I have to go lie down," she says, still holding her head.

I help her over to her room and into her bed. I check her forehead and make sure she's tucked in. I bring another glass of water for her and she takes a few pills with it.

"What are those for, Matant?" I ask.

"I told you before, Faboubou. Pain. It hurts everywhere." She disappears underneath her covers.

I stare at all the foodstuff. Some of it I don't recognize, but there's a list on the refrigerator door: stuffing, cranberry sauce, macaroni and cheese, collard greens, black-eyed peas, sweet potato pie, Haitian rice and beans. Then someone has scribbled at the end of the list: *Don't burn the turkey, Ma!*

The huge, fat turkey is sitting in the sink. I watched Matant Jo just shake some salt and pepper onto it and wondered what else she was planning on doing to it since salt and pepper is hardly enough for a whole turkey. So I roll up my sleeves, wash my hands, and start my magic.

I pound garlic and scallions to add to the turkey. I use cloves, too, and lots more seasoned salt. I soak kidney beans, and wash the rice and set it aside. I've gotten my own ingredients from the supermarket, so I peel cassava, slice plantains, boil the salt out of dried fish. There's fresh and canned pumpkin, and I smile to myself thinking that soup *joumou* is just what my family needs now. I chop carrots, celery, and potatoes. I grate cheese and melt it down with butter and milk for the *macaroni au gratin*.

I spend a long time cutting up the big turkey into small pieces—throwing out extra fat and rubbing it with lemon down to the bone. I boil it for a long time before it's tender enough to fry. I check on Matant Jo now and then, and she only mumbles that everything smells good. Pri tries to come in, but I stop her. I'm at peace here in this kitchen—seasoning, chopping, and stirring pots. I pour every prayer and blessing into the dishes. I hum over the food as if my songs and words will be a protective magic. Chantal tries to come in, too, but I only let her taste the rice and beans since that was her one request. She offers to set the table. I make sure to cover all the pots so that my Thanksgiving meal is a surprise.

I let the warmth of the house wrap around me. I let the scents of my food fill me up with nothing but joy, because this moment is like a hug from God.

Matant Jo has come out and is alive again—dressed, hair and face done, and smiling bright. She looks at me and mouths, "Thank you."

We stand around the table and Pri grabs my hand. Chantal

grabs my other hand. We're all holding hands now and I smile even brighter because I see that my beloved aunt and cousins pray, too.

"God," Pri starts. "I think our cousin, Fabiola, being here is the best thing that ever happened to us. For real."

They all make a sound that lets me know that they agree, and something wells up inside me as if it's been sitting there all along waiting to be set free, and I cry. It's a hushed cry—not like a storm, but like a drizzle.

"It's like she was supposed to be here all this time," Pri continues. "Like she should've never left when she was a baby. And I wonder sometimes what it would've been like if she and her moms stayed . . . if we stuck together like family."

The light drizzle has become hard rain and I cover my face as I cry. Chantal reaches over to hug me. Donna comes over, too. Soon, my cousins are all embracing me and my tears are now a thunderstorm.

"Fabiola," Matant Jo says, and I hold my tears for just a second. "My dear sister, Valerie . . . she's strong. And strongheaded. I know she is fighting to get to you . . . to get to us. And we are fighting for her, too. So today, we are thankful for you. We are thankful for her."

I sniff back my tears; I hold back everything because my aunt is lying. She is not fighting for her sister. If she was, my mother would be here right now. But I don't say anything because my cousins' arms are around me. And Pri cuts through the thickness of my anger and sorrow with one of her jokes.

"Fab, if this food isn't good, we will straight up eat you. Just lay you down on that table and nibble on your bones like *Silence of the Lambs*," Pri says.

"That's nasty, Pri," says Donna.

I pull out the warm turkey from the oven and place it on the table. It's still covered in tinfoil, so I uncover it, and each one of my cousins and my aunt shriek, yell, and cry at the same time as if they've just seen the most terrible thing in the world.

"Fabiola! What the fuck did you do to the turkey?" Pri shouts.

Donna is covering her mouth, Chantal starts laughing, Matant Jo is shaking her head.

"What, what, what?" I ask. "What happened?"

"You weren't supposed to chop it up and put it in sauce!" Pri cries.

"I guess we're having Thanksgiving Haitian style," Chantal says.

I stare at my masterpiece of a turkey—the turkey I spent hours cutting up into small pieces and frying to perfection— the giant breasts, the wings, the legs are all well easoned and resting in a nice spicy tomato sauce full of sliced peppers and onions.

"You gotta be kidding me," Pri whines.

"Hey, sit down," Matant Jo says. "It will be delicious. Appreciate what you have, Pri."

"Wait a minute," I say. "You wanted me to cook the turkey just like that? With salt and pepper and put the whole thing in the oven?"

"Well, you were supposed to add stuffing, then put it in the oven," Matant Jo says.

"But it would be so dry. You wanted that big, dry thing just like that?"

"That's how we do it around here, Fab," Pri says. "Dry-ass turkey and thick-ass gravy."

Still, my cousins eat my stewed turkey, my rice and beans, cassava fritters, fried plantains, and the best one of all, my soup *joumou*. By the time they're on their second plates, the jokes start again, and the laughter, and the lightness.

Then there's a knock at the door and my heart jumps. My cousins and I all look at one another. But Donna winks at me and she's the first to head to the door. Pri follows her.

"My man Kasim!" Pri shouts.

And I freeze in my seat. I have a piece of turkey in my mouth and I'm not dressed properly. I don't have on a bra and the weave in my hair is starting to look like a fuzzy hat. Matant Jo giggles. Before I even think of running upstairs to change and fix my face, Kasim is standing in the kitchen with a smile and a bouquet of flowers.

I chew really fast and stand to take my flowers, but he gives them to Matant Jo instead.

"Oh, thank you so much, Kasim," she says, and kisses him

on the cheek. "Do you have brothers? I need one for each of my girls. And a sister. A sister for Pri." She giggles.

"Thanks, but no thanks, Ma," Pri says, and pulls out a seat for Kasim. "Ay yo, Ka? Your girl done chopped up the turkey and threw it in sauce. Ain't that the most Haitian shit you have ever seen in your life?"

"No," Kasim says. "I've had jerk turkey on Thanksgiving with a Jamaican family I know. Shit . . . Oh, excuse me, Jo. My family boycotted Thanksgiving 'cause my father didn't want to celebrate the white man's holiday. So we had salmon and bean pies when I was little."

"White man's holiday?" Matant Jo says. "Then what's a black man's holiday?"

"Payday!" Pri shouts, and everyone laughs except for me and Chantal.

"You ignorant ass," Chantal says. "What about January first, Ma? When the Haitians got their independence. First independent black nation in the world. That's a black man's holiday. That's what soup *joumou* is for, right?"

Matant Jo shrugs and doesn't answer. So I answer Chantal's question. I tell them about our famous pumpkin soup and Pri reminds me that the pumpkin was supposed to be for pumpkin pie. And the sweet potato that I boiled was supposed to be for sweet potato pie.

Then Kasim says, "Dray's mom makes the meanest sweet potato pie, right, Donna?"

Donna doesn't answer. So Kasim keeps talking about food, his family, and Dray's family, who is like his family.

But him being here has not changed anything. No doors have opened since I've learned about my cousins' drug dealing. Do I hand Dray over to the detective even though he wasn't responsible for the girl's death? And even though he's like family to Kasim?

I must've been sitting there staring into nowhere, because Kasim's hand is on my shoulder shaking me and asking me if I'm okay. I snap out of it.

After the meal, Chantal tells me and Kasim to go into the living room so they can clean up. I excuse myself to go change instead. Then Kasim asks to use the bathroom. We're both headed up the stairs when Pri yells, "Don't stay up there for too long, y'all!"

I make sure the bedroom door is closed while he uses the bathroom, and I change into something more dressy and put on a bra. When I come out, he's right there and says, "Hi."

We stand in the doorway for a moment, and we both know that it's the first time we're alone in a house. Not quite alone, but almost. I start to step around him to get downstairs but his eyes wander into Chantal's room.

"Hey, what's all that?" he asks.

I turn to see my altar—the statue of the Virgin Mary, the tea candle, the bottle of Florida water, the beaded gourd, tin cup, and white fabric. "My prayer stuff," I say.

"Damn, you're like a hard-core Catholic?" he says.

"Yes and no. It's Vodou."

"Voodoo? Oh, I get it now. You put a spell on me?"

"No, that's not real Vodou. We have spirit guides—our *lwas* are like saints and I pray to them for help. And I offer them food in return—candy, rum, and other things. Don't you pray?"

"Used to. With my moms. I grew up Muslim. Kasim means 'divided amongst many' in Arabic. Will you pray for me?"

"Yes, of course. Always."

He eases both his hands toward my face, pulls me in, and kisses me deep, deep.

Cher *Manman,*

It's beginning to feel like you wanted it this way.
Maybe you sent me ahead, and you made it so that you
wouldn't come with me—that you would return home to
Haiti and leave me here in America. If you had told me
to go alone, you knew that I would never agree to it. But
this is how you raised me, Manman. You raised me to be
like another part of you—another arm or leg. Even as you
kept telling me that I'm becoming a woman, you never let
me go out into the world to be free. Or maybe I took the
place of the sister you left behind, or who left you behind.
You raised me like this, so I cannot go on with my own life
without you. You can't go back to Haiti. You have to come
to this side because this new family of mine is both familiar
and strange—just like how I am American by birth and
Haitian by blood, bones, and tears. Familiar and strange.
Manman, your nieces sold drugs. Your sister loaned
money to drug dealers. And Uncle Phillip was killed because
of drugs. If what you've told me is true, that this kind of
madichon runs in the family, then what sort of prayers,

songs, and lwas *will remove this* madichon—*this curse?*
And if what you've told me is true, that the lwas *will show*
up all around me—in both things and people—then I am
surrounded, I am supported. And with the help of Bondye
and his messenger, Papa Legba, the giant gate leading you
home will soon open.

I will make it so.

Kenbe fem. *Hold tight.*
Fabiola

TWENTY-FOUR

BECAUSE OF MY new hair and clothes, no one knows that I've come from Haiti only a few months ago. I fit in like a well-placed brick. We're in a giant gymnasium with hundreds of other teenagers. Our high school is playing against another school in a big basketball game. I don't know the rules of the game, but there are so many cute boys that I don't even care to pay attention to the ball or the score. These boys are not like the scrawny broomsticks back home in Haiti. They have muscles and they move like ocean waves up and down the court. I'm sitting between Imani and Daesia as they point out which boy is the cutest. For a moment, I forget about Kasim. Only for a moment.

Pri and Donna come over to the bleacher seats in front of

us. I glance at Imani to make sure she's okay because Donna sits right in front of her and tosses her fake hair back so hard that it hits Imani's knees. Without thinking, I gently shove Donna's head and say, "Excuse you!"

She turns around and asks, "What?"

"Your hair hit Imani," I say.

Donna glances at her and says, "Oh, did it? My bad," and tosses her hair so that it hits Imani again.

I'm about to tap Donna, but Imani stops me, shakes her head, and mouths, "It's not worth it."

Pri is sitting next to a girl and they laugh and talk as if they are more than friends. I wonder if this is Taj. I tap Pri on the shoulder, and when she turns, I motion toward the girl.

"Oh, Taj, this is my cousin, Fabulous," she says. "Fab, this is Taj." Pri is a little different—the edge in her voice is gone as if she is smoothing out everything about herself to impress this girl.

Taj turns to shake my hand. Her whole face smiles. "Nice to meet you, Fabulous," she says. "I heard a lot about you."

They look good together and I can't help but wonder why Donna has not had the same taste in picking out a good boyfriend. I shake the thought of Dray from my mind because I want to enjoy my friends and this basketball game, but I spot Kasim waving to us from the bottom of the bleachers. I smile big and bright and wave back. I can't hide it. I really am happy to see him. Soon, he's trying to make his way up past the crowded seats to get to where we are. I ask Imani to scoot over, and when I look back up, I see Dray coming up with Kasim.

I tap Donna and point in their direction. She doesn't do or say anything.

Dray, with his eye patch and gold cross, holds his hands out and calls Donna's name. "You gonna leave me hanging like this?" he says.

Other people shush him and tell him to get out of the way.

"Yo, mind y'all fucking business!" he yells to no one and everyone. "Ay yo, Donna?"

"I'm not talking to you, Dray," Donna says by the time Kasim is seated between me and Imani.

"Donna, he just wants to talk to you," he says. I nudge him. He shouldn't get involved, and if he is, he should be on my side and on Donna's side. But I don't say this to him.

Two girls get up from next to Donna to make room for Dray. They end up standing by the bleacher steps. Dray doesn't even sit down when he comes over to us, and he blocks me, Kasim, and the people in the rows behind us.

"If this don't show you that I love you and that I'm sorry, then I don't know what will." He pulls something out of his coat pocket. It's a little red box.

Donna doesn't even look his way.

"If you don't take it, I will!" someone nearby shouts. And everyone laughs.

Dray ignores them. And Donna ignores him. Until he gets

down on one knee in that narrow space between the bleacher seats. Dray grabs Donna's hand and kisses it. "I love you," he says.

And maybe I buy into everything he's selling because I can see how his one eye is almost welling up with tears.

"Don't do it, Donna, don't do it," Pri says through clenched teeth. "Just remember what that nigga did to your face." Her leg is shaking and she keeps her fists balled up as if she's holding everything in. She tries to smile around Taj and is trying hard not to let Dray unravel her. Or else she would've been in his face already, I'm sure. Dray opens the box and it's a pendant. And as if everyone in the gymnasium has set their eyes on the little, bright diamond, they all stand up to cheer. I soon realize that it isn't the pendant that makes them cheer; someone on our team has scored a basket.

"Damn, I ain't even see that shit 'cause of this nigga's big-ass head!" someone behind us says.

"Yo, what the fuck did you just say?" Dray is standing up now, looking behind us.

No one answers him except for Donna, who is trying to get him to sit down.

But Dray is too busy looking for the person who said he has a big-ass head to notice that Donna is trying to take the box from him.

"Who the fuck said that?" he yells at everybody.

No one answers him.

"Kasim, find the bitch who said it and bring her over here."

Kasim looks around and I tug at the sleeve of his coat. I can't believe he is ready to do whatever Dray says, but before I can say so, Donna speaks. "Are you serious, Dray? You come all the way out here to give me this cheap-ass jewelry and say how much you're sorry and how much you love me, and then you're gonna turn around and start beefin' with other people?" she says.

"I didn't come out here to get disrespected," Dray says.

"Well, you're disrespecting me. You *stay* disrespecting me."

Then Dray is back down on his knee and grabs Donna's hand. I can tell by her face that she's buying it. Donna is under Dray's spell again. And Pri knows it, too, because she finally stands up and turns Donna around.

"I swear, I will cut you off if you let that nigga get to you," she says.

Donna puts a hand in Pri's face and says, "I got this, Pri."

Dray eases closer to Donna and leans in toward her. He whispers something—sweet things, maybe. Donna is slowly surrendering. I can see it in her body, how her shoulders come down, how her hand moves toward Dray's hand. He's still saying things to her—putting her under his spell. So I call out her name to snap her out of his spell. "Donna!"

She turns to me. "What, Fabulous?" But Dray starts pulling her down the bleacher steps.

I don't know what to say. I don't know how to tell her not to go with him—to break it off for good so she can be free. And maybe, for a moment, I hope that Dray means it this time—that he's really sorry and he loves her and he won't hurt her anymore. There's nothing else to do but to hold on to that hope. But I know it's a lie that I'm telling myself. It's a lie that Donna is telling herself, too.

Donna and Dray leave the gym. Pri watches them, still with her leg shaking. Then she turns to me and our eyes meet. She shakes her head. I shake my head and shrug. It's the first time we both understand each other without even exchanging a single word. Then something in her eyes softens when Taj touches her shoulder. Pri stops shaking her leg and turns back to Taj and the game. Cooler now, almost liquid.

I'm pulled back into this game, to my friends, and to Kasim when he says, "How many times I gotta tell you not to worry about them? They're doing their thing."

"You think that is love?" I ask.

"He loves her. Trust me. I know. But we won't have that kind of love."

Then right there, right in the middle of the bleachers for all my friends and schoolmates to see, he kisses me on the lips, for a long time. If Dray and Donna's love is like a tornado—wild, dangerous, and unpredictable—then this thing between me and Kasim is like the ocean—deep, deep, and as wide as the endless earth.

I can't sleep because Donna has not come home yet. I'm in that sleep-wake place when I hear Bad Leg. Papa Legba has another riddle for me. My ears are wide open while my eyes stay shut. Chantal's light snoring keeps me from hearing every single word, but it's a song I remember from months ago—one of Bad Leg's very first riddles, before I realized he was Papa Legba.

Maybe it has been a few hours, or only a few minutes, but I'm forced back into that sleep-wake space by the sound of a man yelling. The words are hard and come fast. *Shut the fuck up, old man! Mind your fucking business!* I sit up on the air mattress. My head is still fuzzy, my eyes are sticky. Chantal is still asleep. *You don't know what the fuck you talking about!* the voice shouts. I recognize it. So I rush to the window. I see the white car. I see the top of a girl's head standing in front of the house—Donna. I see Dray standing over Bad Leg, who's just sitting on the bucket. Dray shoves his head.

"Was it you all this time? Huh, Bad Leg? You sittin' here pretending you're crazy and shit . . . ," Dray yells.

I don't think. I'm out of bed, out of the room, and down the stairs in an instant. I hear more shouting from Dray, but I can't hear his words from the living room. I don't even put on a coat. I just open the front door. Donna is there and she quickly turns to me. Her tears are glistening on her cheeks.

"You working with the cops, Bad Leg? You a fucking snitch, man?"

I don't step out because Dray's words *working with the cops* are like a giant brick wall that's been placed in front of me. I was going to help Bad Leg. I was going to beg him to become

Papa Legba again and disappear. But I don't want Dray to see me now. I don't have any words for him.

So I whisper to Donna, "Come inside."

She shakes her head and looks toward Dray, who kicks the bucket that Bad Leg is sitting on. The old man is as still as the lamppost above him. Then Dray shoves him in the head.

"Dray!" Donna calls out.

A light from someone's window across the street comes on. A dog starts barking. Dray steps away from Bad Leg. But instead of walking over to Donna, he gets back into his car and drives away.

"Come in, Donna!" I whisper again so I don't wake Matant Jo.

I pull her in. When we're inside, she rushes into the kitchen and heads straight for the freezer. She takes out a pack of frozen peas, wraps it in paper towels, and puts it on her cheek. I turn on the light. She comes over and turns it back off as I try to pull her hand and the frozen peas away from her face, but she doesn't let me.

"I'm gonna tell Pri," I whisper.

She moves the peas away from her face. I can't see anything, so I take her hand, walk her to the fridge, and open its door so I can see with the light from there. The left side of her cheek is red and swollen with still-bleeding scratch marks. It's from Dray's fist and hands. The scratches let me know that Donna was fighting back.

I pull her in and hug her. I hold her for a long time in the dark kitchen.

"You have the battle wounds of Ezili-Danto," I whisper into her ear. "She is a warrior."

"I fight back," she says.

"No, you are not a fighter. You are Ezili's child—the lover. The beauty. Leave him alone. I will fight for you, Donna. I will fight this battle for you." I kiss her on her head and rub her back as she cries and cries.

Then she says, "Please don't tell my sisters."

"I won't have to. They will see for themselves."

My cousins are hurting. My aunt is hurting. My mother is hurting. And there is no one here to help. How is this the good life, when even the air in this place threatens to wrap its fingers around my throat? In Haiti, with all its problems, there was always a friend or a neighbor to share in the misery. And then, after our troubles were tallied up like those points at the basketball game, we would celebrate being alive.

But here, there isn't even a slice of happiness big enough to fill up all these empty houses, and broken buildings, and wide roads that lead to nowhere and everywhere. Every bit of laughter, every joyous moment, is swallowed up by a deep, deep sadness. This is what happens to Matant Jo, who is back in her dark room again. This is what happens to Chantal when she studies so hard and she still has to find ways to pay for school. This is what happens to Donna, who doesn't seem to know the difference between love and hurt. And Pri just fights the choking air. She fights everything.

And in the middle of all this is Dray. And his uncle Q. One I can't handle; the other I can do something about.

So that night, a rage builds up inside me. I am hot red. I am burning coals. I am a sharp dagger and Scotch bonnet peppers in rum—Ezili-Danto's favorite things. But this is only a wish because my mother—the powerful *mambo*—is not here with her songs and prayers and drums and offerings to make it so. But soon she will. I will make it so that at the very tip of my dagger will be Dray's blood. I have to cut him out of my cousin's life for good.

TWENTY-FIVE

IMANI GOT A C on her paper. She didn't care that I saw her essay when Mr. Nolan put it on her desk. Like me, her hair and clothes are different than they were a few weeks ago. But not in the same way. She wears a big sweater over her uniform and a long coat that almost covers her legs. Her hair isn't combed and she doesn't even put lip gloss on. It's like she doesn't care how she looks anymore. So I ask after class when we're in the girls' bathroom, "What happened? I thought this was your best class?"

She shrugs. "I just wasn't feeling this paper, that's all."

"What? You wasn't feeling this paper? I don't *feel* a lot of the papers or the homework, but I still do it. And I get a good grade. You helped me, so I have to help you."

"I don't need your help, Fabiola." She's washing her hands at the sink and doesn't even look into the mirror like all the other girls do.

"Okay. So why don't you come to my house one day?" I ask. I miss laughing and joking with her and Daesia and Tammie. I've been spending so much time with my cousins, and thinking about my mother, that I could use some good laughs. Imani would make me forget my problems, but only for a little bit.

"If I go to your house, then that means that I would have to get a ride from your cousins, and I am not getting in no car with no Three Bees, I mean, Four Bees. Stop trying to make me the Fifth Bee."

"We can take the bus. And we don't have to be in the same room as my cousins," I try to convince her.

"Look," Imani starts to say. But she waits for the last girl to leave the bathroom. "I don't want no drama, but you have to promise not to tell your cousins."

I erase the hopeful smile from my face and step closer to her. "I promise. You are my friend. Now, what happened?"

She picks up her bag from the floor, opens it, and takes out a plastic bag. She pulls out a dress—a black one, shiny, too small, and too tight probably. "Nice," I say, even though I can't picture her wearing something like that.

"No. Not nice," she says. "Fabiola, this was at my front door in a gift box with a note and flowers. I was so glad I got to it before my mother did. She would've kicked my ass!"

"You have a lover, Imani?"

"Dang, you're so dumb!" she says.

"Hey! Tell me what you are saying. I don't understand."

She takes something else out of her bag. A card. She hands it to me. It reads, *Can't wait to see you in this, Gorgeous. Dray.*

"What?" I shout. "When did you get this?"

Imani shushes me. "Please don't tell anybody. I don't wanna start no mess. I just need him to leave me alone."

"How is he going to leave you alone if I don't tell Donna? You saw what he did at that game, right? Did he send you this before or after?"

"It was like a few days ago, before the game. I thought he'd leave me alone since he got back with Donna. But he keeps texting me."

"Let me see," I say, reaching my hand out for her phone.

"Are you kidding me? I deleted everything. I don't want no trouble!"

She takes her book bag and walks out of the bathroom.

I chase her out. "I will make him stop," I say. "I promise he won't bother you."

"How?" she says. "He thinks just because he has all this drug money, and a nice car, and all these friends who will do whatever he says, that he can have whatever girl he wants. You go 'head and try to stop that. He might come for you, too. He probably has."

"I promise I'll help you, Imani. I got this."

I stick to Imani, Daesia, and Tammie as they walk down the block toward the nearby bus stop on Vernor and Campbell. Most of the kids from our school wait there.

Pri texts me.

I tell her I'm at the bus stop.

She says she's coming.

I hear someone calling my name, and I think it's her or Donna. But when I turn around, I see Tonesha with five other girls approaching the bus stop.

"Oh, shit!" Tammie whispers.

"That's her right there," Tonesha says to the girl walking next to her.

The other girl is about my height, my weight, and has on all black. She's wearing a hood that covers most of her face.

"Hey, Fabulous! This is my cousin Raquel. Y'all can talk about Kasim, woman to woman," Tonesha says.

This Raquel doesn't say anything.

So I say, "Okay. . . ."

"You messin' with Kasim?" Raquel finally asks.

"Yes, he's my boyfriend," I say, and wish that I knew a cooler word than *boyfriend*.

"And did you call my cousin a bitch?" Raquel gets closer to me.

"She called me a bitch, too!" I shout. "And she had an attitude!"

"No, *you* have a fucking attitude. So I'ma call *you* a bitch,

252

then." She steps closer to my face. "And I don't care who your fucking cousins are. The Three Bees aren't here to save you. You started this shit. So let's squash it right here, right now."

"Keep my cousins' mouth out of your name!" I shout. I've heard my cousins say this, but it's the first time that I've tried to wrap this curse around my tongue and I say it all wrong.

Tonesha and Raquel and their three friends laugh at me. I hear the kids around the bus stop giggle, too.

I try again. "Keep my cousins' name out of your mouth, bitch!"

Tonesha is the first to step closer to me. "Yo, call me a bitch one more fucking time and see if I don't drag you across this sidewalk just like Dray be dragging your cousin with her cheap-ass weave all over Detroit. Go 'head. Try me."

"And you could keep Kasim and his broke ass," Raquel says. She moves her head so much that it looks like it will fall off. She's so close to my face that I can smell today's lunch on her breath. So the first thing I do is put my hand in her face. She slaps it away.

With that, I am hot red again. I am burning coals. I am a sharp dagger and Scotch bonnet peppers in rum. I am a volcano. I am Ezili-Danto. Everything—Haiti, my mother, my cousins, my aunt, the house, school, Kasim, the detective, Dray, America—comes to a boil: sizzling and popping and oozing hot, red lava. I clench my fist and punch her in the face. She punches me back. Then the punches come fast and hard.

I've been here before—fighting when someone tries to steal my money, fighting when someone tries to cheat my mother out of her money, fighting jealous girls, fighting boys off me, fighting men off my mother. Fighting. Fighting. Fighting.

Someone starts pulling my hair. It's Tonesha. I'm fighting two girls now. And I hear everyone else around me with their "Oh, shit!" and "Fuck her up, Fabulous!" and "Where Pri at?"

Darkness. Not black, but red. Like blood from the deepest part of being alive. It pumps fire—hot, sizzling in the pit of my stomach. I want to destroy her. Destroy them. Destroy everything. I don't even feel my fists pounding on faces, on bodies, the hair being pulled from my scalp, the fingernails across my own face, the pounding on my back. Maybe I punch concrete, too. I don't know because the red is so hot it numbs me. Maybe I'm fighting the wind, this place called Detroit, my cousins and their walls, the prison that keeps my mother, my broken home country floating in the middle of a sinking sea. Then the hot red wraps its fiery hands around my throat, and I can't breathe.

I can't breathe.

TWENTY-SIX

EVERYTHING HURTS—MY HEAD, my hands, my neck, my shoulders. My scalp, ears, and face burn, and Donna is pressing something cold against my forehead. I wish Pri and Donna would just shut up, but they're cursing and asking me too many questions. I can't understand anything they're saying because the hot red color has cooled off and is now a dull pink that makes me just want to rest my pounding head and sleep.

"Fabiola," someone says, and it's not one of my cousins. It's Ms. Stanley, the principal. "We're going to have to speak with your aunt. She'll need to come in next week after your suspension ends."

"But Ms. Stanley, Tonesha instigated the whole thing," Donna protests.

"That's why she's suspended for a whole week. And Fabiola only gets three days."

"Oh, come on, Stan, it wasn't even in school," Pri says.

"You know better than that, Pri. If it involves two students within a few yards of the school, then fighting is grounds for suspension," Ms. Stanley says.

Never in my life have I been suspended. And never in my life have I fought in or near school. My mother would beat me herself, then would have the mother of whoever I fought beat me, too. Then she would call my aunt so she can beat me with her words. So when we leave the school after I'm suspended for three days and we climb into Chantal's car, I ask my cousins, "Is Matant Jo going to beat me?"

"What?" Pri asks. "Beat you? Girl, ain't nobody getting abused at home for getting abused at school."

"You have amnesia now, Pri?" Donna asks. "Second grade after you beat that girl up for taking your Dora the Explorer book bag, you almost got suspended. Ma tore that ass up!"

"Oh, yeah."

"She stopped doing that at some point, though," Donna says.

"Just like you think Dray will stop?" I ask. I didn't mean to say that. But it just rolled out of my sore mouth.

"You know what? Maybe it's a good thing that you just got fucked up," Donna says. "And I know for a fact that Kasim isn't cheating on you. Those girls were testing you."

"And she passed the test, actually. Fab beat the shit outta those girls," Pri says. "You were throwing punches like Mayweather, and going *in* on both of them . . . at the *same* time!"

"For real, Fab?" Chantal asks. "I think you've just been initiated. This just proves that you could hold your own. We've all been suspended for one reason or another. Welcome to the club, cuzz."

"You were suspended, Chantal?" I ask.

"Bunch of stupid girls messing with me all the time. I couldn't throw a solid punch, but I could sure swing my arms like the Tasmanian devil."

Pri swings her arms around all crazy and it makes the car shake. They laugh except for me. I'm still in pain, but I swallow it.

"Were they hurt?" I ask. "Tonesha and Raquel?"

"Damn, Fabulous. Don't you know the rules by now? Keep their name out your mouth. From now on, they're known as Bitch Numero Uno and Bitch Numero Dos," Pri says.

"No, I got one," Donna adds. "Ugly Bitch and Uglier Bitch."

They all laugh, including Chantal.

Donna is laughing so hard that she rolls down the passenger window to get some air.

"Fab, don't think Ma is gonna let you off easy," Chantal says. "When I got suspended, she made me clean every corner of the house. But as for school, I'm just gonna talk to Ms.

Stanley so it doesn't go on your record. She's good with that, as long as you keep your grades up."

"I don't want to go to that school anymore. I want to use that tuition money to help my mother instead," I say, quiet, quiet. "And I think you all can use that money, too."

No one says anything, but Donna pulls out her compact mirror and she turns it so that she sees me in the reflection. I see her, too. Our eyes meet in that little mirror and all I can think of is my duty to her—Ezili-Danto, the vengeful one. But I will fight Donna, too, if she gets in my way, and if she gets in her own way.

"D? You feeling better? Enough to hit up this party next weekend?" Chantal asks.

Donna puts away the compact mirror. "Hell yeah," she says. The swelling in her cheek has gone down and she's mastered the art of hiding bruises on her face with makeup and extra hair extensions.

"What's she gonna roll up in there with?" Pri says.

My ears are wide open now.

"I already got a plan," Chantal says.

She pulls up to a curb in front of an abandoned building. The signs say that it used to be a church, then a liquor store. Or maybe the other way around. I'm not sure which came or ended first, the God or the sin. Chantal turns to me.

"What?" I ask.

"You know you're the Fourth Bee now, right?" Chantal asks me.

"Okay," I say. "What does that mean?"

"You're in too deep," Pri says. "Plus, you beat up a girl, and you got suspended. Not to mention you're all up in our shit now. So you're a Fourth Bee. You're fam, for real."

Pri holds out a fist to me. I don't know what to do with it, so I just slap it.

"No, Fabulous. You're supposed to give me a fist bump."

So I give her the fist bump she asks for, then ask, "What party?"

"Them white kids over at the Park will pay for anything. . . . I was thinking, with all those pills Ma got . . . ," Chantal begins.

"What park?" I interrupt. I want to know and understand everything if they want me to be the Fourth Bee.

"Grosse Pointe Park. Fabiola, just . . . just listen for now, okay? Anyway, I don't want Q hanging this money we owe him over our heads. We've made that much before, and we can do it again with our eyes closed."

"You've made twenty . . . ," I start to ask, but Chantal sends knives at me with her eyes.

"But on one night, though?" Pri asks.

"No. It's just something to do so that he can see we're out here putting our asses on the line to get him his money back.

Even if it's not all of it, it'll be something."

I try to wrap my mind around how much twenty thousand dollars really is. It's over a million dollars in Haitian *gourdes*, and my mother and I received that much and more from Matant Jo within a year for my tuition and living expenses. So I believe them when my cousins say they've made twenty thousand dollars already.

"So we're gonna steal Ma's pills?" Donna asks.

"She won't even notice, D," Pri says. "It'll be good for her to get off them shits anyway."

The drive back home is longer and quieter because Chantal doesn't put on any music. Something heavy sits between me and my cousins. I wish I'd never found out about their drug dealing. I wish that the detective had never asked me for anything. I wish my mother had never been detained. I wish, I wish, I wish. Enough wishing. There is nothing else to do but to walk through the doors that are opening for me. But this one with my cousins is locked with a key. This is the information I could've given to Detective Stevens if it had been Dray doing the selling. But no. It's my cousins. My family. I won't give them away like that. I would be giving myself away, too, because now, I'm the Fourth Bee.

I let my mind wander as I stare out the window. I notice how much wider the skies are in Detroit. There are no hills or mountains or valleys. In Haiti, behind the mountains are more mountains. But here, at the end of every road are more roads.

And slowly, it seeps in—like water on a boat. I have an idea. It's fuzzy at first. I sit up in my seat and find something to focus my eyes on so I can think. It begins to sharpen. It becomes clear.

"Well, did you kick her ass?" is all Matant Jo says when she finds out about the fight. She's come out of her room just to hear all the details. She doesn't yell at me; she doesn't threaten to not pay my tuition, or send me back to Haiti.

"Hell yeah! Or else she wouldn't be my cousin," Pri answers for me.

"Still, fighting is not gonna solve anything," Chantal says as she wraps a bag of frozen broccoli in paper towels for me to put on my forehead. "You want to be the kind of chick who no one even thinks of fighting."

"I think she got the message loud and clear. No one fucks with the . . . what? The *Four* Bees!" Pri slaps my back so hard that I bite my tongue.

Now everything hurts even more.

I don't eat anything and am stuck on the couch in front of the TV for the rest of the evening. Kasim texts me that he's already heard about the fight. He's working now and promises to call me when he gets out. But I fall into a deep, heavy sleep and my whole body simmers down, then cools, and I am myself again.

I ask Chantal to take me to Kasim's job before she picks up Donna and Pri. It was the first day of my suspension and I'm

261

beginning to feel less sore from the fight. I have to use this time to plan. I know exactly what I have to do.

"Make sure you bring some books with you," Chantal says. "And don't get him fired."

I'm at a table by myself and Kasim has brought over a croissant and hot chocolate.

"I'm on my break, so I can chill with you for a hot minute," he says, and takes a seat right in front of me.

I take a sip of the warm chocolate. "You never make it sweet enough," I say.

He starts to get up to bring sugar to the table, but I grab his arm. "It's okay. You're enough sweetness for me."

He laughs. "You want a corn muffin to go with that cocoa? 'Cause that was kinda corny, Fab."

We're quiet for a moment. Then he reaches over to touch my still-bruised face. "I heard you fucked up Tonesha and Raquel. Damn. Obviously they don't know nothing about no Haitian revolution. Y'all don't play when it comes to fighting."

"That was not a revolution, Kasim. They were disrespecting me, and Raquel told me that she wanted to be with you," I say.

He laughs. "For real, though, they were fucking with you. And you didn't see how butt-ugly Raquel is? I have standards, Ms. Fabulous. There's a bunch a girls out here who will pop off at the mouth just to get a reputation. She would've never stepped to Pri or Donna with that mess. Just 'cause you're new and you got an accent and you're cute, she thought she could fuck with you. And I swear, I'll check both Tonesha and Raquel when I see them. I'm sorry you had to go through that."

I grab his hand and bring it close to my face. "So is this real?" I ask.

"I don't know. What's real to you, Fabulous?"

"For one, my name is real."

"All right, *Fabiola Toussaint.*" Then he takes my hand in his and breathes into it. The warmth travels up my whole arm. "You feel that? That's real." He leans in and kisses me on my sore cheek. It's a mix of pain and sweetness, and I take his hand again and hold it near my face.

Before he leaves the table, he says that Dray will be dropping something off, then he has a surprise for me after he closes up. He kisses me on the lips.

I step outside so that he and his coworker can wipe the tables, mop the floor, clean the machines, and count out the register.

Dray's white car is already parked at the curb.

It's drizzling and cold. It feels like rain, but when the drops hit my face, they're as sharp as needles. It's raining ice. I stand there and make sure that Dray sees me with his one eye. But he doesn't roll down the window to let me in. Soon, Kasim will be out. I need enough time with Dray alone, so I walk over to the white car and tap on the window. He unlocks the doors instead of rolling down the window. I open the door and step into the dark place. It smells like weed again, so I inhale to take in everything about this car, this Dray, this moment. Manman says that in order for the *lwas* to help us, we sometimes have to embody them, let them mount us so they take over our thoughts. We become them so that we can move as they would move.

Maybe I am a little bit like Baron Samedi now, so I ask, "You have some weed?"

Dray laughs. "Some *weed*? Why don't you ask your man to hook you up with some weed?"

"He doesn't know I smoke," I say.

"Oh, you trying to hide shit from your man, now? Don't do that. That's how me and Donna got into this mess we're in now."

I think of bringing up Imani and how he hits Donna, but I don't. That door will lead to somewhere different. I know exactly where I want to go, so I say, "There's a lot of shit I hide from my man."

He laughs. "Yo, shorty. You for real? I'm the wrong person you need to be saying that to. Kasim is my boy." He pulls something out from a little compartment between the seats.

"So. Donna is my cousin. What happens between you and her is your business. But you have to leave my friend alone. Imani doesn't want you."

"But that's between me and Imani, though."

"No, it's not. If you try to bring Imani into this, then it's you, Donna, and Imani."

"Yeah, and ain't no *Fabulous* up in that mix, either. So what are we, in junior high school now? Imani can't speak up for herself?"

"She's scared that Donna will want to fight her. Imani is not that kind of girl."

"And that's what I like about her," he says.

"And that's why you should leave her alone. She doesn't want any trouble and she doesn't want you. Or else she will tell everybody that you won't leave her alone when you already have a girlfriend. You don't want your business out in these streets, right?"

"Oh, I like how you think. Now, you need to convince your other cousins to mind their own business." He hands me the marijuana. It's the length of my pinky finger, and smaller than my mother's cigars.

"Don't tell Kasim," I say.

"Why not? Kasim wouldn't mind, trust me." He pulls out a lighter from his coat pocket.

I let him light my weed or cigar, whichever it is, because I can't tell anyway. I've tried cigarettes before, but would never try one of my mother's cigars during a ceremony for fear that one of the *Iwas* would mount me by mistake. I bring it to my lips, pull in the smoke, inhale, and let it out. I watch as the swirl of cloudy curlicues dance before me.

"Damn, you're sexy," Dray says, almost whispering.

I glance toward the windows of the café. They're fogged, so

I can't see what Kasim is doing now. Still, time is moving and I've only got the key in the door. "I like your eye patch. You remind me of someone I know back home."

"Oh, yeah. An old boyfriend?"

"Yeah," I lie. "He used to help me out a lot." I inhale again, tilt my head back, and exhale.

Dray reaches over and brushes my cheek with his knuckle. "You're smoking that joint like an OG. I like that." Then he turns his whole body to me. "Fabulous, what the fuck were you doing at my house that day?"

"Your house?"

"Q's. My spot."

"That's what I want to talk to you about," I say. My throat and the inside of my nose start to tingle, but I try my best to hide it. I give him back the weed. "I need money, Dray."

"Oh, shit. What you got in mind?" He takes a hit from the joint, rolls the window down, and flicks it out onto the street. Then he scoots over to get closer to me.

"No, not that kind of money," I say, moving closer to the door. "My mother is in trouble. I need money to pay a lawyer."

"Why don't you ask your crazy-ass cousins? Matter of fact, your even crazier-ass aunt."

"I don't want them to know. My mother is being detained in New Jersey. She wants to give up and go back to Haiti. My aunt wants her to go back, too. She says there are no jobs in Detroit, so what's the point?"

"She ain't lying."

"But I want her here with me. I *need* her here with me. I want her to meet Kasim. I really, really like him."

"Can't help you with that, sweetheart. I don't know what makes you think I look like a fucking bank."

"That guy I said you remind me of? Zoe Pound," I lie.

"Zoe Pound? That Haitian gang down in Miami? What you know about that, Miss Fabulous?" He is turned to me fully now. The lock on the door has clicked open.

"I know a lot about that. And they are everywhere. Miami, New York, Boston. Some other places I've never heard of. But not in Detroit."

"Damn right not in Detroit. Them niggas would have a whole lot of competition." He eases back in his seat and looks behind me toward the café.

"My friend Baron, he is a big, big shot in Zoe Pound. He helped me and my mother a lot. But he can't do anything now that I'm on this side. But I need to help him, make some connections for him."

"First it's money, now it's connections. Just spit it out, Fabulous." He moves his hand closer to me, but I don't move my leg.

"I know you sell drugs, Dray. I know some rich kids like to buy drugs at parties. It's the same way in Haiti. I heard some girls at my school talking about a party in Grosse Pointe Park. Do you know about it?"

"Yeah. Go on." His hand moves closer and now it's brushing against my thigh.

"They want something called . . . I don't remember the name. We call it something different in Haiti. But it's drugs."

He laughs, but doesn't move his hand from off my thigh. "Yo, you sound real crazy. You know how hot the Park is right now? You can't just roll up in here fresh off the boat, talking about 'I know this party where you can sell drugs.' That shit sounds crazy to me."

I quickly glance over at the café. Kasim and his coworker must be finished cleaning by now. Time is slipping from me. So I reach over, take Dray's face with its black eye patch and sharp lines, and kiss him. It's a shallow but wet kiss, not like how I kiss Kasim, of course. He is frozen in his seat and I feel as if I've just inhaled his power.

I'm back in my spot when I say, "You don't know anything about me. You don't know what it's like to scratch the walls around you and hope that there is gold on the other side because there is nothing else for you to dig through to make a decent living for yourself. The boys I know back home, they don't just sit around and wait for charity to drop useless coins into their hands. They find a way to live, to breathe. So I know you, Dray. I know that you have the fire that Kasim doesn't have. If you have what these girls want at this party, then sell it. If you make money, give me a portion. Twenty percent. I can use it to help my mother. And if you want, I can connect you with some of my Zoe Pound people. They don't play small games. They are big-time. That's it. It's not complicated."

Dray licks his lips as if to hold on to the taste of me for a moment longer. Then I follow his eyes to the front of the café. Kasim and his coworker have come out. While his back is turned to pull down the gate, I quickly get out of the car so that he doesn't see that I'm in the passenger seat. Once I'm out, I exhale long and deep. My head feels light and heavy at the same time. I want to spit out the marijuana from my breath and the taste of Dray from my lips. But I swallow and let them fill my body as if I've just eaten his soul. Before Kasim turns to see me, I whisper to myself, "Shit you do for fam."

But then I hear the window on the car coming down behind me. When I turn, Dray says, "Five percent."

I almost agree, but I remember that I'm still in battle, still in character. "Fifteen," I say.

Kasim comes over and gives me a hug. Then he leans into the passenger-side window to talk to Dray. "Give us a ride to my car. I parked in the garage around the corner," he says.

He opens the backseat door to let me in. When he slides in next to me, he says, "Damn, Dray. You smoking up the car while I got my girl in here?"

"Fabulous and I got a deal. She's cool with that. Ten, right?"

"Yes, I'm cool with that" is all I say.

"Ay yo, Ka? That's wifey right there, son. You got my blessings," Dray says as he pulls away from the curb. Our eyes meet in the rearview mirror. He winks at me and smiles.

"Thanks, bro," Kasim says, and kisses me on the cheek.

When we get out of the car, Dray gives Kasim a package—a thick yellow envelope. In Kasim's car, he tucks the envelope underneath the seat and asks, "What were you talking about with Dray that makes him call you my wifey and shit?"

"Oh, nothing," I say.

My heart is lingering somewhere in the deepest part of Dray's underworld, and from this point on, I will have to claw my way out.

After Kasim drops me off, I run up to the bathroom, turn on the shower so no one can hear me, and pull out my phone.

"I have something you can use," I tell Detective Stevens.

"Oh, yeah? I'm listening."

"When can I get another phone call with my mother?"

"Another call might be tricky, but I can help speed up her case. Now what do you have for me?"

"There's a party. He will be there."

"He's free to be wherever he wants. We can't pick him up again on bogus charges. He's onto us. We need something that'll stick. We're getting pressure from the Park residents. We're putting pressure on DPD. Nothing's happening. Now, what you got for me?"

"He's going to be selling drugs."

"He will have drugs on his body?"

"Yes. If he's not at the party, then you can't arrest him, right? But if he is at the party, then he's there to sell drugs."

"Okay. But Fabiola, you gotta be careful."

"I am fine. I am strong and brave," I say.

"I see. Good job," Detective Stevens says.

I hang up the phone. The bathroom is hot and steamy now. *B* is for brave, I think.

TWENTY-SEVEN

THAT NIGHT, I pretend to wake up from a bad dream. I toss about on my mattress, even though my body is still sore from the fight. Then I sit up and breathe heavy. Chantal can't see me yet, but I get myself ready for the role. I'm a good actress.

"Chantal!" I whisper-yell. "Chantal, wake up!"

She groans.

"Chantal, you can't go to that party!"

"What?" she whispers.

"You can't go to that party. Something bad will happen."

She sits up. "What are you talking about?"

"It's in Papa Legba's song. The doors have to open just right. You can't try to knock down closed doors."

She leans over her bed and throws something at the opposite wall. It makes a loud bang. "Pri. Donna. Wake up. Come over here." She whisper-yells, too.

Nothing.

She turns on her lamp, reaches for her phone, and dials a number. I can't believe she's calling them from next door, but someone answers.

"Come in here. Wake Pri up," Chantal says.

No one comes into the room. Then Chantal calls again. We hear shuffling next door.

"If that was Dray calling, Donna would've been downstairs already," Chantal says.

Pri and Donna shuffle into the room and they both plop down on Chantal's bed, yawning and rubbing their eyes.

"Tell 'em what you just told me, Fab."

"You can't go to that party."

"Because . . . ," Chantal says.

"Bad Leg . . . he's Papa Legba, and he says to beware."

"Wait a minute," Pri says. Her voice is like sand. "Was this in a dream, or did you hear him say that shit?"

"Both," I lie.

Pri gets up to look out the window. "Oh, shit. Turn off the lights. Turn off the lights!"

Donna turns them off and runs to the window along with Chantal.

"Is that nigga looking straight at us?" Pri says.

I ease up from the mattress, clenching my jaw from the soreness in my back and arms.

"He's there?" I ask. "He's still there?"

"What's up, Bad Leg?" Pri says into the closed window. Then she turns to me. "What? You want us to go down there and ask him if we should go to that party?"

"She already told you he said not to," Donna says. "Right, Fab?"

I nod.

"You're into that voodoo now, too?" Pri asks, and goes over to turn on the light.

"Pri," I say, "this is not the 'voodoo' you see in movies. This is the stuff my mother practiced back in Haiti. She is a *mambo*, a priestess. This is how we pray. We see the magic in everything, in all people. And this Bad Leg has been singing songs and no one listens to him. I listen. And the more I listen, the more they make sense."

Donna comes over to me and sits on the mattress. She touches my cheek and it hurts. "Ezili-Danto," she whispers. "I get it."

I hold her hand there and press it hard against my face so I can feel the pain. Donna knows, and I remember. "Ezili-Danto," I whisper back.

"I'm not going," Donna says. "If Fab doesn't think it's a good idea, then I'm not getting mixed up with no bad juju."

"Bad juju? The fuck?" Pri says.

Chantal is quiet. She goes back to her bed. "All right. Fine. We'll think of something else. That place will be swarming with cops anyway."

I watch as Chantal slips back under her covers. She knows and remembers. She believes what I am saying.

The twins are back in their room, Chantal is snoring, and it's dark and quiet again. This time it's not Papa Legba's words that are swirling around in my head. It's Chantal's: *That place will be swarming with cops anyway.*

This party will be in Grosse Pointe Park, where Detective Stevens works. She asked for proof that Dray is selling drugs in Grosse Pointe. She will get her evidence.

I thank Papa Legba, and Ezili-Danto, and God, and all my other spirit guides who have yet to reveal themselves to me, and I fall into a deep sleep.

TWENTY-EIGHT

KASIM PARKS HIS car in front of a big blue-and-white house with the words HITSVILLE, U.S.A. across the top. It's the Motown museum. He's been playing those songs on the drive here, singing the words out loud as if he wrote them himself for me. Everything is about love and his heart and his girl and his world. I dance and laugh and I am a balloon going up and up into the wide blue sky.

I'm too focused on his lips and smile and eyes to listen to his lessons on Motown and a man named Berry Gordy who started it all. Then we drive around a place called Lafayette Park that he says used to be called Black Bottom. Two tall and wide buildings stand as if guarding the place. Then we drive through a place called Indian Village, where I finally get to see the beautiful American mansions.

"That's my house right there," Kasim says as he slows the car down in front of what looks like a castle.

"So why are you not stopping the car so we can get out?" I ask.

He laughs. "I'm just messing with you. You're supposed to tell me which one is your house."

I look around. They are all different sizes and shapes with wide lawns and gates. I point to a big white house at the end of the block. There's a tall black gate surrounding it, and maybe whoever lives there is a superstar. "That's my house."

"A'ight. I like your house better. When can I move in?"

"No. Not until we're married." I laugh.

"Oh, you're one of them chicks? Gotta make it legit. I feel you."

"Where's my ring?"

He starts searching his coat pockets, the glove compartment, and all over the car. "We gonna have to go to the pawn shop right quick."

I laugh.

We drive out of that fancy place and back to the west side, where he parks in front of a short yellow building called a Coney Island.

"I can't believe your cousins haven't taken you here," he says when he opens the door.

I soon realize that this is like a pizza shop or a McDonald's for Greek food. He orders baklava for me, and I am so hungry that I steal a piece from the bag when he's not looking. He turns around and catches me chewing and I laugh, spitting the piece of baklava out onto the floor.

"Gimme that." He laughs, grabbing the bag from me. "I see I can't trust you around food."

We take our meals to go and drive to his neighborhood, Conant Gardens, and to his block, Norwood Street.

"Make sure you tell your cousins where you are," Kasim reminds me when we reach the street lined with wide lawns and brick houses. "I don't want them coming over here to beat me up."

I'm at a boy's house. I'm at Kasim's house. And there aren't any adults here. Kasim's mother is out with her friends, he says, and my mother would have a heart attack. A text from Pri warns me to keep my legs closed and my pants up. Donna sends hearts and kisses. Chantal only suggests that I be home before midnight.

Kasim takes out our dinner from the big paper bags. "Now, don't you go picking out nothing from off that hot dog. You leave it right there in that bun along with the chili, mustard, and onions. You about to take a bite out of Detroit right here!" He unwraps all the food and sets everything on plates for us.

He takes his first bite from the hot dog and eats as if he's never had food in his life.

I'm too slow with my hot dog. So he picks it up and helps me take bite after bite. He wipes the corner of my mouth with his knuckles. I smile and chew and giggle and cover my face.

"It's good, right? You like it?" he asks.

I nod.

"I like you," he says.

"I know," I say with food in my mouth. Again, he wipes the corner of my mouth.

His house is bigger than Matant Jo's. His block is nicer, too, with lots of big houses and even bigger driveways for the nicer cars. Some houses are empty, too, but the windows are boarded up and their dry grass is low and still kept neat.

"What kind of job does your mother have?" I ask while I'm eating French fries.

"She works for the city. Medical billing. She's responsible for the money hospitals make," Kasim says.

"Does she make a lot of money?" I ask.

"No. But it's honest money, that's for sure."

Guilt settles in my stomach. I can't say that for my aunt or cousins. And now, even me.

A big, L-shaped couch takes up most of the living room, along with a big TV, but smaller than the one we have at home. We watch a funny TV show, and then another show. Kasim keeps his arm around me the whole time, and slowly, he pulls me in for a kiss.

This is not our first kiss, of course, but it feels brand-new. Maybe it's because I have my boots off and my feet are curled up under me on the couch, and his arm is around my whole body. I sniff the bare skin of his neck—a mix of soap, sweat, and hot dog. I kiss it. He shrinks away from me.

"Don't do that," he whispers.

"I'm sorry," I say.

"No. Do that, but don't do that," he says.

So I kiss his neck again. Then he kisses mine, and I don't shrink. I melt.

He stands up and pulls me up with him. He takes my hand and walks to a room next to the living room. He turns on the light and nothing but blue, black, and gray fills the space. The walls are a deep blue, the covers on his bed are a plaid mix of blues. His carpet is gray and his furniture is black.

Before I get a chance to look around, Kasim's arms are around me and his lips are touching mine. Soon, our bodies are so close that we are one person.

And then, I am the color pink. If hot red is for anger and rage, then pink is the color of a soft burning—hot enough to light up the dark corners of sadness and grief, but cool enough to be tender, innocent, open. I let myself sink into Kasim as he pulls me toward his bed. He is soft and gentle. I am like syrup again. And all the walls around me, everything that has blocked my joy these past few months, oozes, trickles, and melts away.

Only skin, muscle, and bone separate my heart from Kasim's heart. I'm so close to him that I can feel it beating against my own chest. Both his arms are wrapped around me, and his leg is stretched out across my bare thighs. It's as if he has swallowed me whole with his body. It's a place so warm and so bright that I swear we must be glowing from beneath his covers. He nestles his face in the crook of my neck and inhales deep.

"Is this real?" he whispers.

I take his hand and breathe into it. "You feel that?" I ask.

Then he presses his body against mine and pulls me in. "You feel *that*?"

"Yeah," I breathe.

Time melts around us. And maybe this bed and his sheets and his room dissolve into nothing. It's just us here. Nothing else matters. Nothing else exists.

Until my phone rings.

It's Chantal calling. Midnight. I don't pick up.

Slowly, we gather the world around us and ease back into the present.

I put my clothes on and he changes into something different. Before we leave his room, we hug and hold each other for what feels like forever.

He kisses my forehead.

"I'll take a beatdown from your cousins for bringing you home late," he says. "It was worth it."

"I am your back," I say.

"Don't you mean you *have* my back?"

"No. I *am* your back."

"For real, Fab?"

"Yes. It's real," I say.

KASIM'S STORY

Dray used to call me a mama's boy. My moms used to roll up to my school and plant a fat wet kiss on my cheek for everybody to see. She said it was to let all those teachers know that I was loved. But I caught hell for it from my boys.

Mama still kissed me on the cheek and rubbed my bald head when I was in high school. Now, don't get me wrong. I wasn't spoiled or nothing. She just liked to show me off in public. But in the house, you best believe she had me scrubbing pots, cleaning toilets, putting up shelves, and shit. Those were the times I wished I'd gone down to Memphis to live with my pops. There were times when I wanted to straight up hop on a Greyhound and leave Detroit for good when I had to deal with all the bullshit out here on these streets.

I did some dumb shit just so niggas would stop calling me a

*mama's boy. Shit that would break my mother's heart. But that's
what I had to do just to be able to walk down my own block without
being somebody's bitch. That was back in junior high. But by high
school, I had to be able to walk through somebody else's hood and
hold my head up. Truth is, I didn't. I don't like rolling with a bunch of
niggas. You end up doing even dumber shit and paying the price for it.
     But Dray's been lookin' out since I was in kindergarten and he
was in third grade. Once my pops left, it was just me and my moms.
So that's when Uncle Q stepped in. If she had to work late, Q let me
stay over and me and Dray would play video games all night. At
first, my moms didn't trust Q, but after a while, she had no choice.
He was the only man to come through for her. They never went out or
nothing, but Q was like, whatever you need. And I needed a friend.
That's all. Just one good friend. Not a crew, not no gang. Just Dray.
And if Q is like a father to Dray, then Q is my father, too. Never
mind my real father who begged me to come down to Memphis 'cause
he need somebody to pass on that big ole house to. Maybe when I get
married. And have some little half-Haitian revolutionary babies.
Hell yeah. I ain't never felt like this before. I mean, I told girls I
loved them and shit. That's what I do. I love girls. Since I don't
like rolling with a crew of niggas, I stay up underneath a girl all
the time. That shit is soft and warm and safe, feel me? But you . . .
Damn, girl. I'll finish college for you. I'll get a nice government job
for you. I'll save up and buy a house for you.*

TWENTY-NINE

"**NOW DON'T GO** following him around like a sad puppy," Chantal says as she's typing on her laptop.

"What? No way!" I say. I try not to giggle, because I feel guilty that Chantal knows.

"I know you're not. But if I'm right about Kasim, he's the one who'll be following you around like a sad puppy."

"He's coming over soon. He's bringing pizza. Want some?"

"Thanks, but no thanks," Chantal says.

"Why don't you have a boyfriend, Chantal?" I finally ask, because Donna is still in love with Dray and Pri likes Taj.

"Like I said, thanks, but no thanks."

"Is it true? You would make love to a book?"

"Yep." But she can't hold back her laugh. "For real, though,

I hope you never end up in a place where you feel ugly."

"Feel ugly? Somebody told you that?"

"No one had to tell me, I just felt it. And don't give me no 'but you're beautiful on the inside' bullshit."

"No, you are beautiful on the outside," I say.

"Don't give me that bullshit, either. I'm beautiful when I say I'm beautiful. Let me own that shit," she says. Her eyes have not left the computer screen this whole time, but I know she's paying attention to everything I say.

"Okay, then you are ugly."

"Thanks for being honest."

"Seriously. That's what we say in Haiti. *Nou led, men nou la.* We are ugly, but we are here."

"We are ugly, but we are here," she says, almost whispering. "I hear that."

Chantal goes back to her typing and I stand in front of the dresser mirror with a pair of scissors. I'm ready to cut out this stupid weave. But I don't know where the fake hair starts and my real hair ends. So I call for Donna. In an instant, she's in the room with her own pair of scissors.

"You can't just cut it. That's one hundred percent human hair," she says.

Soon, I'm on the bed as she carefully cuts out the strings that were used to sew the fake hair into my cornrows. When she's done, I'm so relieved to have my head back that I scratch my scalp for a whole ten minutes. I have to hurry up and wash my hair and get dressed before Kasim gets here.

I text him for an exact time, then get into the shower. My body feels brand-new. Every part of me is open and ready to let the world in. I use all of Donna's soaps that smell and look like cake. I spray on her perfumes—I can't decide which one I like best, so I use all of them. My hair is back to normal, and while it's wet, it sits high and round on my head. I use some moisturizing cream to gather it all up, brush it, and pin it into a neat bun. My scars from the fight are fading now, but my face still looks different. Older, maybe. Wiser, definitely.

I check my phone.

8:00 p.m.

Kasim has not texted back. I don't want to seem like a sad puppy, so I don't send a text, either. Back in the room, I stare into the mirror again. I like this me better. No fake hair, no thick makeup, just my clean, simple face and my bun.

I settle on a pair of gray sweatpants because it will be a cozy TV night on the couch. I wear one of Donna's sweaters and notice that the neckline is wider than usual. It's meant to slide off one shoulder. So I let it do that. One shoulder is naked and sexy. I add some oil. Maybe he will kiss me there.

9:00 p.m.

He should've been here by now, or at least called or texted. So I type in, *Hey?* and a sad face. I send it.

I want to take it back because that sad face is the sad puppy I'm not supposed to be. I think of something else to text. Music comes on downstairs. So I type, *Party at the Four Bees house! You coming?* and a happy face. I send it.

I pull out a book from Chantal's shelf to read—something about a brown girl who wants blue eyes. Chantal passes me a bag of potato chips. I don't take any. I want to eat the pizza Kasim brings.

10:00 p.m.

Fab, I won't be coming tonight.

Are you okay?

Just got some business I need to handle right quick.

It's so late. You working?

Maybe I could hit you up after I'm done. Will you be up?

I'm going to sleep. I will talk to you tomorrow.

Cool. Can't wait to see your face again.

I leave him alone to his business, throw the phone on my mattress. I grab Chantal's bag of potato chips and look through Kasim's last text. I read the line *Just got some business to handle right quick* over and over again.

What business would Kasim have tonight anyway? Tonight is the night of the party. Tonight is when Dray is supposed to go and sell those pills. I shake the thought from my head, but now that the thought is here, I cannot shake it away.

I quickly run out of the bedroom and down the stairs.

Pri is still on the couch watching TV. I grab her coat from the closet and throw it on. The cold wind almost knocks me off my feet when I open the front door. Chantal is right behind me, but she just stands in the doorway.

"Fab," she says. "Why are you running out of here? Where you going?"

I ignore her. When I reach the corner, Bad Leg is there, thank goodness. He looks different. He's all dressed up in a black suit and bow tie. And sunglasses. He's wearing sunglasses just like Dray.

"Papa Legba," I say, and pull the coat's hood up over my head. "Did everything go as planned? Eh, Papa Legba? Did everything happen the way it should?"

When Papa Legba speaks, my legs begin to shake:

Cupid's bow and arrow
aimed straight for the heart.
Tears shed from sorrow
tearing everything apart.

I take slow steps back to the house as Bad Leg sings this song while laughing and coughing and starting the song over again.

"Fabiola, get in the house! It's cold as fuck out here!" Pri yells from the doorway. Chantal is standing next to her.

"What's going on, Fab?" Chantal asks. "Why are you running to Bad Leg?"

I come in and close the door behind me. *Cupid, arrow, heart, apart.*

"What's wrong with your face?" Pri asks. "You look like you've just seen a zombie."

Donna comes to the door to see what's wrong.

I check my phone. Kasim has not texted again. So I call him.

No answer.

"Fabiola?" Chantal says. "What's going on? Why you acting all crazy?"

I call again. No answer.

"Donna, where is Dray?" I ask.

"I don't know, and I don't care," she says.

"Can you call him, please?" I'm out of breath. My heart is a heavy bass. My stomach is a slow-burning fire pit now.

"Why?" Donna asks.

"Yeah, why, Fabiola? Why do you want her to call Dray right now?" Chantal asks.

"Is he at that party? I need to know if he's at that party." I can't get all the words out right. My body wants to do something else besides be in this house. I go back into the room and start to look for another sweater.

"What party?" Chantal asks. "The one in Grosse Pointe? Why would he be at that party, Fabiola?"

"Yeah, why would he be at that party?" Pri asks.

Pri is repeating everything Chantal is saying and it's driving me crazy. I want to yell "shut up." But I don't want to say another word.

So I call Kasim again. Nothing.

Chantal grabs me by the shoulders. "Fabiola, why would Dray be at that party? Why do you keep calling Kasim? And why are you talking crazy?"

They all surround me now, and I'm about to explode.

"What did you do, Fabiola?" Chantal asks, with her eyes and her lips trembling.

Chantal drives so fast that I can't even stand to look out the window. I'm in the passenger seat and I keep my head down on the dashboard, and for a good ten minutes, I forget to put on my seat belt. Their voices beat on me—pounding and pounding. I explain everything—Manman, the detective, what I told Dray. Pri wanted to punch me. She was so close, she was right there in my face—she could have. She didn't. But she called me every single dirty name she could think of. Chantal is as quiet as death. My head is spinning. Everything is spinning and moving so fast that it makes me sick to my stomach.

My cousins hate me now.

"I'm gonna call him," Donna says really quiet.

"Don't fucking call him, D," Pri says.

"What if he's there with Kasim? They'll both get locked up."

"Dray is not stupid. He's not going anywhere near the Park. You know that. Too bad *she* couldn't figure that out." Pri kicks the back of my seat.

"And even if he was there, he'd know better than to have anything on him," Chantal says. She's been calm, even as she speeds and swerves around cars on the highway.

"So that leaves Kasim. You hear that, Fabulous?" Pri leans toward my seat and yells, "Your man is gonna get locked up 'cause of your dumb ass!"

"Pri, calm down and sit back," Chantal hisses.

I want to remember Papa Legba's words now, but it all starts to feel and sound crazy. I need a prayer, a song, but everything now is too real—just as it was during the earthquake in Haiti. Even as people threw their heads back and screamed to God for help, the concrete and dust kept falling. That's how it is now. If I were to call on God and my *lwas*, would they hear me? Would they see me in this speeding car holding my head and stomach and begging that Kasim is not arrested?

Something hits me as Chantal exits the highway and the car slows down. *Mesi, mesi, mesi,* I say to myself, to my *lwas*, to God. I don't have my phone, so I ask to borrow Chantal's.

"Who are you calling?"

"The detective."

"Nope! Hell no! You fucking kidding me?" they say all at once.

"I will tell her not to arrest Kasim. She knows he's not Dray. It's Dray she wanted."

"Is that what *you* wanted? You wanted Dray to get locked up so you could get your mother?" Donna asks.

I close my eyes and hang my head low because I've betrayed her. Even with everything that Dray has done to her, she still loves him. So betraying Dray was like betraying Donna.

"Yo, I cannot believe this bitch here!" Pri says.

"She will listen to me. She will not arrest Kasim. And Dray won't be there for her to arrest him," I say softly, trying to satisfy Donna.

"Fabiola! Do not talk to the detective. Do not talk to cops. Do not talk to lawyers. That's just how it is out here. That's code. No more snitching!" Chantal says. Her voice is louder and harder.

I shrink. I am small. I am nothing now. Where have you taken me, Papa Legba? What is this gate you have opened? I try to make sense of everything Chantal was trying to explain to me back in the house. If Kasim is selling for Dray, he will still get hit with the charge, as she said. And the cops will only get to Dray if Kasim snitches.

The houses are bigger here—the lights on their lawns, walkways, and porches are brighter. The Christmas decorations are on the roofs and all over the wide and tall trees that tower over the curving roads. This must be the place where dreams rest their heads. I want to press my forehead against the window to get a better view of the houses, but it's dark and I'm still shrunken in my seat.

Until lights pour into the car—spinning blue and red siren lights from the police cars and ambulances. My insides sink.

"What's the kid's name, Donna? The one throwing the party," Chantal asks as she slows down the car.

"Bryan Messner. Is this Buckingham Road?" Donna asks.

Chantal looks up at her phone that's stuck to the dashboard. "Yep. Shit. It's hot out here. Cops are all over the place."

"We can't be anywhere around this party with all these cops, Chant," Pri says. "Let's just go home."

Chantal parks the car far away from the swirling lights in the distance. "No, hold up. If Kasim is still there and nothing went down, we'll take him home with us. Let's just wait it out," she says.

But I don't want to wait it out. I want to run out of the car and toward those lights, so I unlock the door. But Chantal grabs my arm. "Don't even think about it."

"Why don't I go?" Donna asks.

"So they could be like, 'That's the bitch who sold me the bad pills'?" Pri says. "See? We can't even get into the party, so now what?"

"I'm calling Dray," Donna says.

"So he could figure out that your cousin set him up?" Pri says. "And find out that we went to Q behind his back."

I'm tired of listening to them talk. So I open the car door, step out, and slam it shut behind me.

"Fab, where you going?" I hear, but I keep going.

Everything in my body feels tight and heavy as I walk away from the car, as if my skin and bones know that something is not right. I hear a car door slam shut behind me.

"All right, look," Chantal says when she reaches me. "We're gonna pretend we're going to the party. Okay? Don't ask for Kasim. Don't even mention his name. Let him see us first so that he's surprised and it looks like a coincidence that we're there."

I agree, and we walk down the street arm in arm—like a united front. This is how me and my mother would walk the streets of Port-au-Prince at night. If anybody wanted to take on one of us, they'd have to take on both of us. But we are not in Port-au-Prince. We are in Grosse Pointe Park. The air is lighter here, like how the air is freer in the rich hills of Petionville. But this dark free air feels dangerous, as if it knows we're not supposed to be here, that we don't belong here.

I want to say sorry to Chantal. I want to ask her why, with all that money, they never bought a house here. I want to ask her why, with her all her brains, is she selling drugs. I want to talk, to sing, to take my mind off what I may have done to Kasim. But we're getting closer to the swirling lights. They hurt our eyes, so we both raise our hands to shield our faces.

There are people everywhere. We come closer to a car with

the word POLICE stretched out wide across its side in big blue letters. A cop is approaching us. My stomach tightens and I squeeze Chantal's hand.

"Young ladies, you can't come here," the cop says.

"We're going to Bryan's party," Chantal explains. Her voice and words are different again. I'm not sure if she is answering the cop or asking for permission.

"Party's over. You live around here?"

"Yeah. Over on Three Mile Drive. We walked here."

"Three Mile Drive, huh?" He looks us up and down as if we are dirty. "Let me see some ID."

"Okay," Chantal says, and digs into her jean pocket. "It's my high school ID from University Liggett. I don't have anything with my address on it. Did something happen over there?" Chantal says with her soft, easy voice.

The police officer looks at the ID card and then at Chantal and back at the card. He hands her the ID and motions for us to turn back around. "Go home, girls. Party's over and there's nothing for you to see here."

"Okay, thank you, officer." Chantal takes my hand and starts to walk back.

I take a few steps with her toward the car, but something tugs at my insides. I can't go back home. I have to know what happened with Kasim. This is all my fault, and there's something back at that party that I have to fix.

I pull away from Chantal and run. I run past the cop. I run toward the blue and red siren lights. I run toward the crowd of teenagers.

"Hey! Hey! Stop! Stop!" the cop's booming voice shouts behind me.

But I don't stop.

I hear Chantal calling my name. But I don't stop.

I only slow down when I reach the crowd. My heart races. The air around me isn't enough. I can't breathe. Something is wrong. I can feel it.

Then I see her. Detective Stevens is standing right there, a few feet away. Her eyes are stuck on me as if she can't believe that it's me, that I'm here.

She opens her mouth to say something, but she stops. Then she starts again, "Fabiola . . ."

Behind her, I catch a glimpse of cops unraveling a long stretch of yellow ribbon with the word CAUTION. The word goes around the whole ribbon and reminds me of one of Papa Legba's warnings: *Beware the lady all dressed in brown.* The word *beware* echoes in my mind as Chantal pulls me away from Detective Stevens.

CAUTION. *Beware.* CAUTION. *Beware.*

Again, I run. I run past the detective. I run between the people standing around the yellow tape—some whispering, some covering their mouths, others shaking their heads. I push them out of the way because that yellow tape is like a magnet. I'm pulled to it because there is something there. I know it. I just know it.

The first thing I see is a white sheet. I remember seeing this before. The earthquake. White sheets. Bodies. White sheets over bodies. A sea of white sheets. A mountain of bodies.

But here, there is only one white sheet. And one body.

I feel as if something is rising out of the earth. But the ground doesn't shift. It's my bones that are quaking. My knees are weak. I'm closer to the white sheet—to the body. And I know.

I know that body.

It's Kasim.

It's Kasim's body under that white sheet.

I fall to the ground.

I become the earth and I crack on the inside. The fault line spreads and reaches my heart.

I am the one broken now.

Kasim means "divided amongst many" in Arabic.

I remember those words. His voice is clear in my head.

So when I am completely split in half, I wail. I scream. I yell out his name over and over and over again. *Kasim. Kasim. Kasim.*

I try to crawl toward the white sheet. Toward the body.

I'm on my hands and knees, and the cold ground beneath me is as still as death. It doesn't rumble. It doesn't crack. But I do.

Someone picks me up from off the ground and whispers, "Get out of here, Fabiola." It's the detective. I let myself go in her arms. But she is too weak to carry my load.

"You killed him?" I say with my tiny weak voice. "You shot him?"

"Not me, Fabiola. You have to get out of here. Get her out of here," the detective says to Chantal.

My body still trembles. It's as if my soul wants to let go of it, to climb into that space where Kasim is lingering. He wants me there with him, I'm sure.

Chantal's hold is even weaker. She almost falls with me. I can't walk on these broken legs. I can't hold on to my soul with this broken body. *Kasim.*

Still, we make it back to the car. I fold myself into the back-seat next to Pri.

"The police shot Kasim," Chantal says, quiet, quiet.

When I hear those words, I become undone. So I cry and scream and hold my belly as if I am giving birth to all the misery and pain that has ever walked the earth.

Kasim is the earthquake and he has shattered my heart into a million little pieces.

THIRTY

WE ALL CRY. We are a chorus of silent tears, tiny whimpers, deep guttural wails, and sharp piercing shrieks.

The drive back home is slow, as if we are inching our way through muddy dirt roads. Chantal leans in close to the steering wheel, wiping away tears every few seconds. She has to see straight for us. She has to be strong for us.

I unravel. I am the loudest. I am the shrieking one. It all pours out of me like a billion knives. I can't stop. I can't think straight. I only dump sharp, slicing, painful wails out into the car. The windows are closed. None of it escapes into the cold, wild air.

"Shit! Shit, shit, shit, shit!" Pri says over and over again when we drive up to the house.

I quiet down to a whimper. Through the windshield, I spot Dray sitting on the steps to our house. I don't react. I have no emotion left for him.

"How the fuck did he find out so quick?" Pri says through tears.

"I'll go talk to him," Donna says, sniffing back her tears.

"No," Chantal says, calm. Too calm. "He's not here to talk, Donna. Kasim must've had some of Dray's other boys with him and they got away. Dray knows exactly what went down. We need a plan."

"Why the fuck are you talking about a plan?" Pri shouts. "He sees the car. He's staring right at us!"

"Call Ma, then," Donna says.

"She hasn't been picking up all night. I bet Q got something to do with that."

"Q? What did he do to her?" These are the first words I speak since leaving Grosse Pointe. They almost choke me.

"He won't hurt her, but he'll keep her out of the way."

"Turn back up Joy," Pri says. "Let's get the fuck outta here!"

"No," I say, and open the door to the car.

"Fabiola!" Chantal calls out.

But I'm already in front of the house. The car doors slam behind me as my cousins join me. I step right in front of Dray with my fists clenched, my body aching, and my heart broken.

He's not wearing his eye patch, and for the first time, I see that there's a balled-up scar and a narrow sliver of white where an eye is supposed to be—as if someone had dug it out and left only a ghost of an eye.

I start to say something, but he cuts me off.

"'Cause of you, my cuzz is dead. How? Tell me something now! I wanna hear it from your mouth," he hisses.

"Dray, baby . . . ," Donna starts to say as she walks up next to me.

Dray puts his hand up to Donna's face but keeps staring at me. "This has nothing to do with Donna. Nothing to do with Pri or Chant. This is between me and you. Talk. Now!"

"Dray, I . . . you . . ." The words are stuck in my throat.

"She ain't got nothing to do with this!" Pri shouts. She pushes me out of the way and I bump into Chantal. "Whatever beef you got, you deal with us."

"Go inside," Chantal whispers to me, handing me her keys. "Go inside!"

"She ain't going nowhere, son. Stay the fuck out here," Dray says. He opens his coat, but I can't see what he's showing them from where I'm standing.

"Nah, bro. Deal with me, nigga! I'm right here. I'm right here!" Pri shouts in his face.

Chantal shoves me out of the way and I stumble toward the steps. My cousins have surrounded Dray and are yelling in his face, telling him to leave me alone and deal with them, all of them, instead. As I watch him from behind, he is calm like Baron Samedi.

Baron Samedi. Ezili. Ezili-Danto. Ogu. Les Marassa Jumeaux. Papa Legba.

These are my guides. I need them now. I have to call on them. If there ever was a time that I needed to pray, to pour libation, to ring the bell, to rattle the *asson*, to sing a song so all my ancestors and my *lwas*, so God can hear me, it is now!

I rush into the house, up the stairs, and into Chantal's room. My hands are trembling. My whole body shakes. With only the streetlight from outside pouring through the window, I search for my lighter and tea candle. I've added more things to the altar over the past couple of months—candy for Ezili and the *Marassa*, a Scotch bonnet pepper for Ezili-Danto, a razor blade for Ogu, and since I haven't been able to find cigars, a cigarette taken from Mantant Jo's room for Papa Legba. These are all offerings to the spirits, and in return, they will help me.

But a loud banging makes me drop the *asson*. My heart jumps when I hear loud footsteps coming up the stairs.

Dray.

I don't even have time to close the door and lock it before he bursts in and pulls me out of the room by my hair, then the hood of my coat, then my arms. I scream. I kick. I fight. I scream louder. My cousins have come up the stairs, too, and they're pulling my body in the other direction. Crying. Screaming.

"Let her go! Please, let her go!"

"Fuck outta my way!" Dray shouts.

I cry and scream from the very bottom of everything that makes me alive. I pull from life itself and dig for the loudest, most painful cry in the whole world, because my body is being dragged down the stairs and the skin on my back burns from scraping against the carpet. I dig my fingernails into his hands and arms. I dig for flesh and bone and maybe, if there is one, for a soul. Then I grab the banister while my body is stretched out on the stairs. Chantal is above me, pulling my leg, trying to keep me upstairs. My head burns. He's ripped out my hair, maybe. I don't let go of the banister. But he pulls my fingers off, bends them back so that they almost break.

And still, I make that sound from the God place. I beg for my life because it must be Death that awaits me at the bottom of the steps, in the living room, in this house.

"Fabiola, Fabiola. Don't fight, Fabiola. Don't fight," someone says through tears. Donna. Her voice is worn now, as if it's been stretched too thin.

But there is nothing left to do but fight. I keep grabbing the banister and screaming. He pulls my fingers back, then he grabs both my arms. He wins. I am at the bottom of the stairs. Still, I fight. I kick. I scream.

There's a hard blow that makes me numb. Darkness swallows my face, eats my thoughts. The pain pulses throughout my body and makes me weak, makes me surrender. I hear words and voices and cries as if they are far away, sealed tight in a jar.

"Get the fuck up!"

"She can't. You kicked her!"

"Fab? Fab? Get up. Please get up."

Another jolt of pain. In my face. It echoes in my head like church bells.

"Don't fucking kick her in the face! You want her to talk? Don't fucking kick her in the face!"

A sound—flesh against flesh. A scream.

"What the fuck, Dray! What the fuck! Pri, Pri! Get up."

"Dray! Stop! Please! Stop!" It's Donna's voice, chopped into broken pieces.

"Shut the fuck up! Yo, wake her up. Wake her up or I swear to God I'm gonna light this whole house up!"

"Fabiola? Fabiola? You gotta talk. You gotta explain yourself. If you can hear me, try to get up."

"Kasim," I manage to say, because the taste of iron fills my mouth, the same mouth he's kissed.

"Yeah, yeah, yeah! Yeah, bitch! Kasim. Say his name one more fucking time. Kasim." Dray's voice breaks.

It sounds like a giant wall has cracked, and soon it will come tumbling down.

With my head still like the bottom of a beaten conga drum, I stand up. I hold on to Chantal, and when I'm on my feet, my head spins. I spit my iron blood in his face. "Kasim," I say again.

He doesn't wipe it away. "Yeah, my fucking brother, son! That was fam, son! My brother. He was all I got. All I got!"

His voice is shaking. Dray's wall is cracking, splitting down the middle.

I can see him now. Close, so close. Something is in his hand, but I don't dare turn my head to see because I might fall again. I can think of no other words besides his name. "Kasim" is the only breath I can breathe right now.

"You gonna fucking come in my car, and kiss me, talking about how you need money for your mother, bitch?" He paces around me.

Chantal pulls me close to her, but I free myself. I want to be like a tree, a concrete pole—unbreakable.

That thing in his hand is up by my face now.

A gun. That thing in his hand is a gun.

"Dray, baby. Baby, listen to me." Donna with her broken voice.

"Shut up, Donna! Shut up. You had something to do with this, D? Huh, Donna? The way you left me hanging like that? You had something to do with this?"

"Dray. No, baby, no. I swear. Baby, I would never do that to you."

Donna is a river. Her cries flow into every corner of the house. Chantal only breathes heavily, as if this space is slowly wrapping its hands around her neck. Pri is a ball of fire—still, steady, waiting. She stands close to me, ready to catch me if I fall.

"Huh? Answer me!" Dray yells, and his spittle reaches my face. "You want your ten percent now, Fabulous? Huh?"

My cousins plead. Their words are prayers to the walls, this house, this corner.

He presses the gun against my pounding head. The tears from my eyes are a waterfall. My bones are rattling, and maybe even the blood that flows from my heart is running toward safety, trying to get out. Get out. But I am as still as a pole.

"Dray. Not here, not now," Chantal says. "We didn't know. We didn't know."

"Yo, fuck you! Shut the fuck up! I'm talking to this bitch right here. Huh, snitch? You gonna fucking snitch? You don't even know how this shit works out here in Detroit. You gonna talk to cops, bitch?"

I can feel his whole body shaking from how he holds the gun against my head. His wall is tumbling down.

I remember walls. I remember concrete. Whole cities can seek vengeance, too. And even the very earth we stand on can turn on us. I remember the rumbling sound of falling walls, of angry earth. And maybe the dead rose up out of the ground the day my country split in half, and the zombies, with their guardian, Baron Samedi, leading them, forced their way out of cemeteries in search of their murderers.

I will do the same. By the grace of my *lwas*, when his walls come tumbling down for good and he kills me tonight, I will do the same.

I am not afraid of dying. Death has always walked close—an earthquake, a hurricane, a disease, a thief and his knife. If

Death owns half of my aunt, then I will sell my whole self to it.

My mother will know where to reach me.

So I say, "Do it, Dray. You want to kill me, do it!"

"Fabiola! No! No!"

My cousins try to pull me away, but I am steel, too.

I squeeze my eyes shut.

A click.

A bang.

A burn.

A dark.

A light.

THIRTY-ONE

WHEN THE BIG earthquake happened, I was in a courtyard—
our house with its two floors was on one side, and another bigger house with its wide three floors was on the other side. I was
putting clothes on the line after coming home from school.
Manman had just taught me how to boil water in the big alu-
minum pot over hot coals to pour into a bucket of dirty clothes,
then drop in a bar of indigo soap, and, once the water cooled
off, crouch down around the bucket to scrub the clothes between my hands.

My hands were still too small to make the squishing wet
sound my mother's hands made when she washed clothes. Still,
I was learning. And I was getting better.

I was humming a song. I don't remember which one. My

knees hurt from squatting so low. I stopped for a moment to stand up and wipe the sweat from my forehead with the back of my wet hand, and maybe, I thought, I was dizzy, because everything around me moved. And then there was a rolling sound. I swayed and dipped, and in an instant, the walls around me started coming down. The columns that held the second floor of our house split in half, and the roof surrendered. A long crack eased up on the side of the other house. And soon, the concrete, the stones, the marble tiles, the dancing rebar, all fell down around me.

And it rained dust and screams and prayers.

I was in the middle of it all, standing on my two skinny, ashy legs, with my wet hands. Alive. Unbroken, after all.

My eyes are still shut.

But I am still standing.

Slowly, I open my eyes.

I am not dead.

Dray is.

His body is slumped over the banister, and he slides off, slowly, slowly. Bright red oozes from a hole on the side of his face, near his broken eye.

And I am shaking. I am the earthquake. I can't stop shaking.

My cousins are frozen in place, but their eyes look past me, behind me.

Slowly, I turn.

And there, in the open doorway, is my Papa Legba. Still

with his black tuxedo—torn and old now—his cigar, and his cane. Or a gun. Or a cane. No, a gun. A cane.

I stare. I want to move closer. To touch him. To ask him questions. But I just stare.

And then he sings his song.

Crossroads, cross paths,
Double-cross and cross-examine,
Cross a bridge across my mind.
A cross to bear across the line,
And cross the street across town.
Cross out, cross off,
cross your t's and cross your fingers,
then nail him to a cross as you cross
your heart and hope not to die.

As he sings this, the streetlight begins to shine through him as if he is made of nothing. Slowly, the top hat, the tuxedo, the cane, and the man begin to disappear right before our eyes. He becomes the smoke in his cigar—thick cloudy air blending with the light and cold air.

He's gone again. And I force my aching body to run after him. I hold my head as it pounds and spins. I reach the corner of American and Joy. He's not there. Nothing is here. I want to call out his name. I want to say thank you. But instead, "Kasim" eases out. I turn to the house to see Dray's white car parked in front. I don't want to go back into that house with its dead man and his gun and my blood that is not my blood and their *madichon.*

Chantal runs out to get me and pull me back into the house.

Then Pri comes to stand next to us, next to where Donna is lying over the dead body crying and crying.

And I think, I never got to do that with Kasim, just as Pri says, "We never got to do that with our father."

We all stand there and inhale, exhale together. In one breath.

"Go upstairs. Get a sheet," Chantal says.

I have to step over Donna to get upstairs.

DRAYTON'S STORY

Ain't no way for you to know what it feels like to leave your body when you die. It's not like in the movies, where you just float up into the air. Ain't no floating, white clouds, bright lights, angels singing . . . none of that shit.

It hurts. A bullet to the head . . . it goes straight through and turns into some kind of blow horn for your memories. It wakes up shit you ain't never thought you would remember. And you realize that this shit ain't new—you've been dead before.

I remember running toward sky, some open space, some room to breathe. Freedom. And I wasn't supposed to. So a bullet pulled me back to reality. At that point, death was more real than anything because I remember not owning my own body, my own breath, my own thoughts. In death, you own it. You take back your shit—your body, your thoughts, your past—and you own it.

Even when I'm born again in Detroit, and I'm supposed to be free like the fucking wind, there's still some shit trying to own my life—money and the bullshit jobs my moms had to work, these shitty streets, and this whole fucked-up system. When you remember all the ways you been killed, and how that shit hurt your fucking soul, ain't no way in hell you could shake that off. So I didn't give a fuck about nothing. Niggas out here threatening to take my life, I just laugh and promise to come back when I'm gone. That's why when Q put a gun in my little ten-year-old hands and told me to aim it at that guy with the Detroit Tigers cap, it wasn't even a thing.

It's war out here, son. If my pops and his pops before him been fighting all their lives to just fucking breathe, then what's there for a little nigga to contemplate when somebody puts a gun in his hands?

But my aim was off. My little hands were cold, sitting in the passenger seat of that car. Q was right there next to me telling me to calm the fuck down and aim straight for the Detroit Tigers cap. He was teaching me more about these streets than my pops ever did. But it was all wrong from the start. He got into my head. It messed with my aim.

The blowback made me drop the gun and I missed the guy in the Detroit Tigers cap. It hit a guy named Haitian Phil in the back of his head.

He got into my head. It messed with my aim.

I spent the rest of my life working on my aim and trying to prove to Q that I'm a real G. I never said a word to nobody, not even Haitian Phil's daughter. I couldn't hate Q. I couldn't hate my fucked-up aim. But I could hate that girl for having a dead father whose ghost fucked with me in my sleep, in broad daylight, and even when I was so high, I could hear every fucking cell in my body move.

Everything got into my head—this life, these streets out here, this fucked-up system. They all messed with my aim.

And there's nothing left to do down here where it's dark and empty but wait to go back. That's my one aim.

THIRTY-TWO

KASIM'S FACE IS everywhere. Not just in my thoughts and dreams, but on TV, on the internet, on posters all over downtown. Even on T-shirts that Chantal brings home one day. His ghost is a giant. And it's as if every part of him has been spread all over Detroit and lives in the air, in the water, and in other people's thoughts. His arms and legs reach farther than he ever would if he was still alive. Everyone is talking about Kasim Anderson. People say, "I am Kasim Anderson." They march to the border of Grosse Pointe with his big name and his face on big posters, and they shout, "I am Kasim Anderson!"

I remember Kasim means "divided amongst many."

They say, He should not have been killed.

Other people say, But he was selling drugs.

Some say, But he was running. He should not have been running.

More people say that he deserved to be alive.

I hate the way they toss his name around like that—like a ball in a game. He is dead because we all killed him with our own stupid games. That's what I say, but there is no one around to hear me.

I met his mother. She knew my name. That was all she said, my name. Her words were drowned in tears.

The people at school are quiet around me or they apologize over and over again. Imani hugs me and rubs my back whenever I see her after class.

Ms. Stanley asks me to come into the office one day. Mr. Nolan is waiting there with her.

"We wanted you to come in without your cousins, Fabiola," she says. "We're here for you."

They talk some more, but I don't hear their words.

The teachers know my story now. They know our story— the Three Bees. No. The Four Bees.

Chantal is Brains.

Donna is Beauty.

Pri is Brawn.

I am Brave. No one has to tell me this. I know it for myself.

I slip in and out of class like a ghost. My cousins and I, we fold ourselves and try to become small, small.

We don't go to the protests downtown. We don't talk to reporters when they come to our door. We hide.

The ghosts in the house start to crowd us. We feel them in the walls, in every room.

Kasim is not here. He is with the people—spread out over Detroit, and Michigan, and America, and maybe even the world. Divided amongst many.

No one talks about Dray. His death was not on the news. But he lingers in this house. I feel him by the doorway, never moving with the wind, as if he is stuck there.

Self-defense is the word that has been programmed into me, into us. Self-defense. Even though they found no gun to match the bullet in Dray's head, no one digs for more answers. But some truths are buried so deep, not even the earth understands it.

I had to give a statement. I had to piece together everything about that night, and tell it to a detective man and his notebook. Chantal spoke for us with her high-pitched questioning voice.

They are watching us, Matant Jo says.

They've always been watching us, Chantal says.

I don't have the heart to write my mother. I would have to put everything down in words. So I try and try to call her. The numbers are dead ends. My questions are not answered, but her name is still in their system, they say. Is she in Haiti? I ask. They can't tell me that. Was she let out? I ask. They can't tell me that, either.

Part of me wants to go to New Jersey to find her. The other part of me wants to leave here for good and return to Haiti. Maybe she is there already. Maybe this was never supposed to be home. Maybe I was supposed to be here just to get this Dray out of my cousins' lives.

But what about Kasim? Why Kasim?

Divided amongst many, I remember.

I don't call Detective Stevens. I pray that guilt has swallowed her whole.

So we all move as if we're walking through molasses. Everything is slow and thick and threatens to suffocate us.

A black car pulls up next to me one day, while I'm waiting near a supermarket for my cousins to pick me up. I am not afraid of Dray's people. So I stand there and look directly into the dark windows.

One rolls down. It's Detective Stevens sitting in the backseat.

"Get in, Fabiola," she says.

"No," I say. My bags are heavy. It's almost Christmas and I am planning to cook a small meal of Haitian and American food. I want to carve out a slice of happiness just for a moment so that I don't die in this place. I don't want to talk to her.

"I have some information on your mother," she says.

She disarms me with this bit of truth. So I climb into the backseat with my bags. It's warm and smells like coffee and cigarettes.

Detective Stevens turns to me. Her face is different, or maybe I am seeing her with different eyes. She doesn't smile like when I first saw her. If I'd first seen her with this face—furrowed brows and thin, pursed lips—I would not have trusted her.

She gives me a yellow envelope. I open it. It's cash and a woman's name from the ICE—Immigration and Customs Enforcement.

"She's already started the termination of proceedings," Detective Stevens says. "ICE will drop the charges and release your mother into the United States."

Before I leave the car, I tuck the yellow envelope inside my coat.

Papa Legba doesn't show up at the corner anymore. I don't hear his words. Every now and then, I try to remember one of his riddles, but it only conjures up more regret and guilt. I am superstitious about money now. It is like rainwater here. It pours from the skies. But if you try to catch all of it with wide hands and fingers spread apart—it will slip through. If you try to catch it with cupped hands, it overflows. Here, I will tilt my head back, let it pour into my mouth, and consume it.

We have to become everything that we want. Consume it. Like our *lwas*.

On the morning before we leave to pick up Manman, I help Pri squeeze two suitcases into the car.

It's colder than it's ever been and I'm not wearing any gloves. The skin between my fingers burns. It's cracked and blistered from all the scrubbing and scrubbing. I didn't wear any gloves, either, when I filled buckets with alcohol, bleach, and ammonia, dumped old rags and sponges in, and scrubbed death from the walls and floor of the house. The smell still lingers everywhere and sticks to our clothes and skin, and even our food. So Matant Jo is finally ready to leave this house.

We are all in white. Even Pri has shed her dark clothes and now wears a white turtleneck and pants. I had wrapped my cousins and aunt in white sheets after making a healing bath of herbs and Florida water for each one, and let them curl into themselves and cry and cry. This is what Manman had done for our neighbors who survived the big earthquake. The bath is like a baptism, and if black is the color of mourning, then white is the color of rebirth and new beginnings. Our brown skins glow against our sweaters, pants, and head scarves. We are made new again.

"You got your voodoo stuff in there, Fab?" she asks.

"Pri, you have to treat it with a little more respect. It's not just my 'voodoo stuff.' It's my life," I say.

"So what? Without it you're dead?"

"I don't know, Pri. I've never been without my prayers and my songs. What do you hold on to?"

It's snowing now. The white flakes dance around us as if they are part of this conversation.

"Myself. My family. Hopes. Dreams. Shit like that."

She goes back into the house and I stand there near the car looking all around me. I rest my eyes on the street signs— American Street and Joy Road.

I notice something shift out of the corner of my eye. I turn to see Bad Leg near the lamppost. I start to make my way to him, but someone calls me from inside the house.

It's Chantal.

By the time I turn back, he's gone.

"Get in here, Fab!" Chantal calls out.

The kitchen is almost clean and completely empty. Matant Jo says that the stove and cabinets and even the leather couches will be a gift to the neighborhood. Even if we bolt lock the doors, they will know that we have left for good and will not return.

I start to roll up my sleeves to finish the last bit of cleaning when I hear Matant Jo wail. All of us rush to her bedroom door.

She is standing there, all dressed in white, with boxes and bags on the floor around her. Her fists are clenched; her face is tight and wet from tears. She finally breaks. Her whole body looks as if she is fighting—fighting us, herself, the air around her, this house, this city, this country, maybe. Finally, she rests her head on Pri's shoulder and sobs. "What a life, eh. This is my whole life."

Her daughters surround her. She cries in their arms. And I

watch these girls, my blood, my family, and wonder if there is room for me.

Donna extends her arm out and I slowly walk over. They pull me in. Matant Jo's warmth and pain is the magnet that pulls us all together.

Still, someone is missing. My mother.

We spend the next couple of hours cleaning the rest of the house and bringing out bags of garbage onto the sidewalk. Pri is the last one to walk away after Chantal locks the front door. Matant Jo is the first one in the car. She brings a box of pictures with her and sits in the front seat next to Chantal. She places two photos on the dashboard. One is of her and my mother when they were teenage girls. They are both smiling, wearing blue jeans and T-shirts, and their hair is in thick plaits. The other is of my aunt, my uncle Phillip, and my cousins when they were babies, standing in front of 8800 American Street. Uncle Phillip is holding one baby—Princess or Primadonna, I can't tell—while Matant Jo holds the other baby. Chantal wraps her small arms around her mother's leg as if she is afraid of whoever is taking that picture. Then I see something in the background.

I ask for the picture and bring it up close to get a better look. There, in the photo, in the background, is Bad Leg—Papa Legba—watching over the family since the very first day they moved in.

When the car pulls away from the curb of the house on

American Street and drives down Joy Road, I turn to see Papa Legba leaning against the lamppost with a cigar in his hand and his cane by his side. He turns to me with his white glistening eyes and tips his hat.

I smile and nod and mouth *mesi*. Thank you. He has brought my mother to the other side.

I stare out the window as we drive out of Michigan. I press my forehead and fingertips against the glass. On the other side is the wide, free road. Unlike in Haiti, which means "land of many mountains," the ground is level here and stretches as far as I can see—as if there are no limits to dreams here.

But then I realize that everyone is climbing their own mountain here in America. They are tall and mighty and they live in the hearts and everyday lives of the people.

And I am not a pebble in the valley.

I am a mountain.

AUTHOR'S NOTE

The first seeds of *American Street* were planted in me when I read the *New York Times* article "Last Stop on the L Train: Detroit." The article was about the far-reaching gentrification of Bushwick in Brooklyn, New York, and the migration of its priced-out residents to Detroit, Michigan.

This resonated with me because Bushwick was my first home in America. I was four years old when my mother and I left Haiti to move there. I didn't know it then, but 1980s Bushwick was described as a war zone. While our house on Hancock Street was fairly intact, other blocks were lined with burned-out buildings and open lots littered with torn mattresses and old tires. When I read that *New York Times* article, I kept thinking about the parallels between present-day Detroit and the Bushwick I grew up in. I thought about writing a book that rides the train from Bushwick to Detroit and tells the story of an immigrant girl who, like me, found her way to the other side, out of poverty and chaos.

While working on *American Street*, I pulled from my own memories of living in between cultures, the experiences I had in high school, and the many tragic stories about the violence and trauma that girls have endured. In Haiti, many girls dream of the freedom to live without the constraints of oppression. Yet more often than not, these girls and their families leave their home countries only to move to other broken and disenfranchised communities. I kept thinking about how these girls balance their own values and culture with the need to survive and aim for the American dream.

One girl in particular stuck out in my mind. When Trayvon Martin was killed in Florida in February of 2012, he had been on the phone with Rachel Jeantel, the daughter of a Haitian immigrant. During her testimony in the George Zimmerman trial, I recognized a little bit of myself in Rachel, and in the many Haitian teen girls I've worked with over the years. We fold our immigrant selves into this veneer of what we think is African American girlhood. The result is more jagged than smooth. This tension between our inherited identity and our newly adopted selves filters into our relationships with other girls and the boys we love, and into how we interact with the broken places around us. I saw Fabiola in these girls, and that's how this story was truly born.

Above all, I wanted to give Fabiola a strong cultural connection to Haiti so that she's spiritually grounded when faced with tough decisions. While Vodou is practiced by many in the Haitian diaspora, it still has a negative stereotype in the media as being associated with evil and witchcraft. Vodou has a complex pantheon and mythological system, much like Greek and Roman mythologies. Through Fabiola's eyes, her new world and the people who inhabit it are just as complex and magical as her beloved saints and *lwas*. She infuses Vodou into everything that happens to her. This is the source of her courage, and I think she is more American because of it—this merging of traditions, this blending of cultures from one broken place to another. I remember those rides on the L train with my mother, my broken Bushwick, and graffiti covering every inch of the subway cars. I once saw a young man steal a diamond ring right off a woman's finger. My mother pulled me in close and prayed under her breath. We'd made it to the other side, just like Fabiola, but what was this life? I don't know what my path would have been like if I had grown up in Haiti, but I know this much is true: I would not have told this story.

ACKNOWLEDGMENTS

In Haiti, before a storyteller begins her tale, she asks her audience for permission with a single call, "*Krik?*" Her listeners respond with a collective "*Krak!*" before she can begin. This book would not be possible without a whole village's resounding "*Krak!*" Thank you, dear reader, for allowing me to share this gift of story.

Thank you to my *manman cherie*, Monique, who envisioned a life beyond the sunsets, where I was free to dream up stories. I am immensely grateful for my husband, Joseph, whose unwavering support has allowed me to write down said stories well into parenthood. Our three children are the reasons for everything. My dear sisters, Ingrid and Carine, *merci* for keeping the memory of my beloved Ayiti alive in my stories. Thank you, Theresa and Garvey, for your humor and youthful wisdom. Thank you to my late father, Marcel, a pioneering radio broadcaster whose storytelling genes are hardwired into my blood and bones.

Ammi-Joan Paquette, thank you for always championing my ideas and visions. I am truly honored to have you as a literary agent, and to be a part of the wonderful EMLA.

If these characters have found a home in this story, and this story has found a home in this book, then this book has found a home at Balzer + Bray/HarperCollins. I could not be more proud. Thank you, Alessandra Balzer, for loving this book from the very beginning. Donna Bray, Kelsey Murphy, Kate Jackson, Suzanne Murphy, Andrea Pappenheimer, Kerry Moynagh, Kathy Faber, Caroline Sun, Patty Rosati, Molly Motch, Nellie Kurtzman, Bess Braswell, Elizabeth Ward, Julie Yeater, Sabrina Abballe, Alison Donalty, Mark Rifkin, Renée Cafiero, and Lillian Sun, you've all made my dreams come true.

And thank you to Team Fabulous at Alloy. Hayley Wagreich, you've dedicated so much to this story and these characters; clearly, we've had so many mind-melding moments. Thank you, Natalie Sousa and Elaine Damasco, for capturing the beauty of this story on the cover. She is truly gorgeous. Josh Bank, Joelle Hobeika, Sara Shandler, and Les Morgenstein, thank you for crossing uncharted roads and paving new paths. It has been a wonderful journey.

Edwidge Danticat and the many literary daughters of Anacaona before me, every word committed to the page is in your honor. *Merci*, Merline St. Preux for this seed of a story.

Thank you, Rita Williams-Garcia, Jason Reynolds, Laura Ruby, and Nicola Yoon for your kind and thoughtful words.

Dhonielle, Gbemi, Jenn, Renée, and Tracey, thank you for keeping this sistership afloat with lots of tea, no shade, desserts, wine, and coins!

I am grateful for my beloved Allies in Wonderland, and the whole WCYA program at VCFA, where I discovered that wondrous imaginative play and critical academic study can happily coexist, and that this will be my lifelong work.

Finally, thank you to the many Detroit natives in my circle. Professor Ebony Elizabeth Thomas, you are golden. Your love for this work is palpable. Thank you for opening many doors, namely, Gregoire Eugene-Louis and Dr. Kafi Kumasi.

And to the late Brook Stephenson, thank you for your love of Detroit, and Brooklyn, and writers, and books, and life.